**Former DEA Agent and
Best-selling Author of *Deep Cover***

MICHAEL LEVINE
TELLS YOU WHAT YOU CAN DO:

• Start targeting users, not dealers.

• Begin Tactical Street Actions in conjunction with the police to keep buyers away. The dealers will soon leave.

• Use cameras, lights, loudspeakers, and signs to let drug buyers know you're watching them—and that you know who they are.

• Make sure your child knows what you think about people who take drugs.

• Use shock tactics to warn children about the dangers of drugs. They work!

• And much more . . .

**HERE IS A BOOK DESIGNED TO START A
WHOLE NEW KIND OF WAR ON DRUGS—
AND WIN IT!**

Also by Michael Levine

DEEP COVER

FIGHT BACK

How to Take Back Your Neighborhood,
Schools, and Families from the Drug Dealers

MICHAEL LEVINE

A Dell Trade Paperback

A DELL TRADE PAPERBACK

Published by
Dell Publishing
a division of
Bantam Doubleday Dell Publishing Group, Inc.
666 Fifth Avenue
New York, New York 10103

ISBN: 0-440-50366-3

Printed in the United States of America
Published simultaneously in Canada
September 1991
10   9   8   7   6   5   4   3   2   1
BVG

To my family and friends, I'm sorry. I just can't stand the drugs anymore were the final words of my brother David, written just before putting a bullet through his own brain on February 27, 1977. It was the end of his nineteen-year battle with heroin addiction. I dedicate this book to his memory.

"I just didn't want to lose you as a father" were the words of my daughter Nicole explaining her own victory over drug addiction. I also dedicate this book to her and to the power of love.

To my son Keith, one of New York City's "finest," who faced some pretty rough times and quietly did his thing without ever taking drugs, while many of those around him did.

And most of all to my mom, Caroline Goldstein, who suffered through this drug plague as much as anyone I have ever known.

Contents

FIGHT
BACK

Introduction

This book is for those of us fed up with the lies and false promises of bureaucrats who promise that if we vote for them and increase the funding for their "war on drugs," things will improve; then take our votes and money and do nothing. It is for those of us sick and tired of calling the police about a drug problem and having them say, "I'm sorry, but our hands are tied." It is for those of us tired of hearing politicians tell us that we've "turned the corner" in the war on drugs while we can't turn the corner on our own streets without being accosted by drug dealers or mugged by crack addicts. This book is for those who want to do what the government has been unable to do for almost three decades—take real, instant, and meaningful action to rid our lives of drugs. If the latest Gallup poll is accurate, that means the vast majority of us. It said that the American people are in "a wartime mode"—fighting mad.

If you *are* fighting mad, you are going to love this book.

This book is also for those lucky enough to be living lives *not* directly affected by drugs, and who want to arm themselves with a weapon to protect their neighborhoods, schools, and families.

This book is especially for those most vulnerable to the lies and false promises—those of you trapped and suffering the drug addiction of loved ones. I have been one of you for many years. You need the information in these pages more than anyone. It may be your only opportunity to learn some sobering truths and get the kind of practical advice I don't see available anywhere—advice I wish my own family had had more than twenty years ago.

This book is written with all the energy, emotion, and dedication that kept me going through my twenty-five years as an undercover agent in our phony, no-win war on drugs; my family's fourteen years of suffering through my brother's heroin addiction; and my own struggle in my daughter's five-year victorious battle over drug dependency. Because drug abuse affected me so personally, I used my position as a federal narcotics agent and my involvement with tens of thousands of drug-related tragedies to try and learn as much as I could about the prevention, cause, and cure of drug abuse.

What I learned and what most of you will be learning for the first time in these pages is an alternative approach toward winning the drug war that has already been proven successful—an approach many people with financial, political, and bureaucratic careers that depend on the existence of a war on drugs and a healthy underground drug economy do not want you to know about.

I wrote my previous book, *Deep Cover,* to expose that fraud, and stress how futile it is to pin our hopes on the promises of many of our bureaucrats and politicians whose main concern is their own careers, and whose notions of really winning a war on drugs have long been forgotten.

This is a book for you who are willing to take your

destiny into your own hands, and rid it of all signs of drugs. It will supply you with the knowledge and expertise of some of the most effective police and narcotics agents in the drug war—the *real* experts. It will reveal the methods and philosophies used by civilizations who have quickly and effectively defeated drug epidemics as bad as, if not worse than, ours; and how an enforcement approach derived from their experiences helped a group of federal agents put a notorious drug den out of business, in ten days, when more than three years of conventional, get-the-drug-dealer enforcement methods had failed.

This book contains all the information you need to do it on your own; to show our leaders the kind of drug war that really works; to *fight back* and take your own families, schools, and neighborhoods back from the drug dealers.

The two types of people most clearly responsible for our lost war on drugs are the experts and the druggies. For this book to be successful, the former will often have to be ignored, and the latter controlled and/or rehabilitated. Before going any further each should be defined and certain seemingly irrefutable facts accepted.

EXPERTS

I remember listening to a very famous politician—one of a handful of perennial presidential hopefuls—delivering a lengthy antidrug speech before the press. He went on at great length about "demand reduction" being the final answer to our drug problems, mentioning the phrase eleven times (I counted). One of the reporters asked the politician exactly what demand reduction meant, to which—after a perturbed pause, because he had never been asked, or expected, *that* kind of question—he answered, "We'll leave that to the experts."

The sad thing about his response was that it was accepted by everyone listening, including the reporter who had asked it, as a valid answer. We Americans have an unshakable belief in experts—no matter how much evidence there is revealing them as misguided, ineffectual, and even dangerous. If the media calls them "expert" and/or they have a few degrees tacked onto their names, they *must* know what they are doing. So we place our children in their care, pay their fees, and vote for what they tell us to vote for.

More than two decades ago the "experts" began telling us that the answer to our nation's drug problem was to spend more money for education, prevention, jobs, treatment, rehabilitation, law enforcement, massive foreign antidrug aid and crop eradication programs, and lately, military action. And we, dutifully, followed their advice. Over the past twenty-five years—still following their advice—we have gone from spending millions to tens of billions of dollars yearly in all the programs they recommended. Since 1965 narcotics enforcement has gone from the old Federal Bureau of Narcotics, with 250 agents in the world, to gigantic bureaucratic empires involving huge war-on-drugs budget expenditures by the DEA, FBI, Bureau of Customs, Internal Revenue Service, the Bureau of Alcohol, Tobacco and Firearms, the Pentagon, the CIA, the State Department, the Coast Guard, NASA, and many other federal agencies. Virtually every state in the union has also devoted massive expenditures to narcotics enforcement. New York State alone, for example, had over a billion dollars budgeted in 1990 for *its* war on drugs. Drug treatment has in itself become a giant billion-dollar industry, with some programs charging hundreds of dollars a day per bed and having waiting lists for beds that are years long. Between the federal government and the fifty states we have spent the last twenty-five years like dutiful well-programmed robots putting countless billions of dollars in the hands of experts. Yet the drug problem, by any measure, is worse now than it has ever been.

And what is the latest remedy recommended by the experts? Spend *more* money on *more* of the same programs.

THE BIG LIE

After twenty-five years of being deeply involved in every phase of our country's war on drugs—from orchestrating far-reaching undercover probes into the top echelons of the drug world, to evaluating the efficiency and effectiveness of domestic and international enforcement operations as part of a team of troubleshooters—I got a clear picture of why we're losing and will never win. The basic philosophy of our approach, what I call the "Big Lie," was doomed to failure from its inception and the whole war on drugs converted to a massive, fraudulent boondoggle.

Huge bureaucracies, created to eliminate drugs from our society, recognized that by doing so they were enforcing themselves out of existence. The Drug Enforcement Administration, Bureau of Customs, Pentagon, CIA, FBI, Coast Guard, and scores of other agencies, on both the federal and state level, receive either all or substantial amounts of their budgets under the guise of "war on drugs." At this writing, with the cold war over and the communist threat no longer what it used to be, our Pentagon has made public the blueprint of massive military involvement in the drug war. If American citizens could accomplish, as the people of two other cultures have successfully done, the elimination of drugs from their society, these huge bureaucracies would either be out of business or lose massive funding, power, and influence. Thus a continuing, albeit futile, war on drugs is very much in their interests.

How are American taxpayers conned into the continued funding of so obvious a failure? The Big Lie.

For the past three decades law-enforcement experts have convinced us that by going after the drugs in source countries; chasing the dealers, smugglers, and drug barons; making bigger and bigger seizures of drugs, money, and property (a supply-side enforcement philosophy), we would in some way affect the amount of drugs consumed by Americans; that by virtue of the threat and use of our law-enforcement and military might, we would deter people from growing drugs in their countries and selling them in ours. In this endeavor we have lost countless lives and spent many billions of dollars, all the while *knowing* it doesn't work. History has clearly shown us that as long as there are significant populations in the world depending on drug crops for their daily survival, and correspondingly significant numbers hungry enough for drugs to spend hundreds of billions of dollars, neither law enforcement nor military will serve as a viable deterrent.

"We know it doesn't work," said one of DEA's top bosses during a high-level planning session at the agency's Washington, D.C., headquarters during November 1987. "But we sold the operation up and down the Potomac." He was talking to me about "Operation Snowcap," our latest paramilitary effort to stop cocaine at its various South American sources—an operation that has since been expanded to include full-scale military operations. "If [Operation Snowcap] fails, DEA goes down the tubes," he continued, " —so it will succeed, one way or the other." He went on to say that it no longer mattered how many huge drug seizures were made, or how many "Mr. Bigs" we arrested, he and the people who had conceived of the operation were well aware that the whole effort was futile. It was, and is, a gigantic perpetuation of the Big Lie.

The Big Lie extends downward from the federal government into our cities, towns, and communities, where politicians and bureaucrats, to win elections and fund their local bureaucracies, still con Americans into believing that going after the suppliers of drugs—from street-corner pushers to international drug barons—is the way to remove drug trafficking from their communities.

It just ain't so.

It doesn't work, and most of them know it. And if they don't know it—take it from a twenty-five-year veteran of narcotics enforcement—they shouldn't have their jobs.

American citizens trying to organize themselves to effectively eliminate drugs from their communities should be aware that the Big Lie, on the lips of their local politicians and bureaucrats, is something they will surely encounter; something that the information in these pages will help them to overcome.

DRUGGIES

(Drug consumers; hard-core and casual)

One would have to search long and hard to find people more self-centered, depraved, and antisocial than druggies: yet our politicians, bureaucrats, and experts persist in painting them as "victims." The fact is that, insofar as all drug-related crimes are concerned, it is the druggie who is victimizing us. It is *he*—not the drug dealer, the smuggler, the Medellín cartel, or all the Manuel Noriegas of this world—who is responsible for the spread of drug abuse.

Part of the druggie psyche is to turn others on to drugs,

either just for the "fun" of it (which accounts for the vast majority of cases), or to support their addiction. Of the thousands of druggies I have dealt with, I have yet to meet one who did not get his first drug experience from either a druggie "friend" or an acquaintance at some social gathering. Casual users are the ones most responsible for the recruitment of new druggies. They don't *sell* drugs but give the stuff away on dates, at parties, at the office, whenever the notion strikes them, mindless of the tragic consequences their "gift" might have. Not only are they the most responsible for the rapid spread of drug abuse, they are also the major source of the $200 billion spent yearly on drugs.

PART I

Drugproofing Your Community

1
Identifying the Enemy

Before you can take meaningful action to remove drug trafficking from your community, along with the crime that accompanies it, it is important that you now reject what our drug-war leaders and "experts" have been telling us are the causes of our national drug problems for the past three decades—*the Big Lie.*

Of all the nations affected by drugs, we continue to be the only one fighting an overseas war "to stem the flow." And according to many experts (including Jack Lawn, the ex-chief of DEA), even if, by some miracle, we stopped the overseas drug supply, there are enough homegrown and homemade drugs to immediately fill the gap. We are already the world's second largest marijuana growers and the largest producers of speed (methamphetamine) and dozens of other drugs produced in clandestine laboratories. Yet, in spite of this, our leaders continue to adhere to the same failed programs and policies—policies based on the perception that the growers, smugglers, and dealers of drugs constitute The Enemy, while the users are hapless victims who must be protected. It's a popular perception that wins elections, but all the same, it's a lie.

What is truly astounding is that there have been two cultures, China and Japan, that have quickly (each in less than three years) overcome drug problems as bad as or worse than ours, by targeting the *real* enemy—the drug consumer. And our leaders haven't even *begun* to examine ways of adopting their successful solutions to our problem.

I realize that a lot of people get very upset with the suggestion that we follow policies of other nations—particularly those of Communist China—so, before going any further, I will hasten to add that I am *not* advocating that we follow their precise solutions. America has the greatest thinkers in the world. I believe that by adopting the principle of using our resources to control and/or rehabilitate the drug user, instead of continuing our present emphasis on law enforcement and a militarized drug war, we can quickly bring our drug-abuse problem under control in an American-style "cure." A cure that can be accomplished without adding a single law to the books or changing one comma in our Constitution. A cure that can be begun in the home, in the school, and the community—with or without the help of government. And that is what this book is all about.

TWO SOCIETIES THAT DEFEATED THE *REAL* ENEMY

"Therefore, when the People's Republic of China eradicated opium addiction over the past two and one-half decades, the United States took no notice of that significant fact. This was a reflection of our foreign policy of pretending that [they] did not even exist . . ."—Congressman Charles D. Rangel (D) New York, Congressional Record, Monday, October 6, 1975, E5261.

China[1]

Mainland China has the dubious distinction of having had the worst drug epidemic in the history of mankind. By the end of World War II China had a staggering *70 million heroin and opium addicts* (more than one third our nation's population). Compare this with the May 1990 estimate of fewer than 2 million hard-core drug users in the United States.

In 1949, when the Chinese communists drove Chiang Kai-shek from the mainland, they made their first priority the suppression of *drug addiction*—not supply. In addition to all the cultivation laws and the bans on possession and sale, similar to ours, the Chinese main antidrug thrust was against the users. All addicts were required by law to register themselves with the government for treatment. All those who did not register—unless they could demonstrate that they were drug free—were either forcibly interned in treatment centers or sent to prison. Either way, they were removed from the drug market.

The enforced hospitalization program was accompanied by a government-sponsored antidruggie propaganda program. The user was depicted as more an enemy to an orderly society than the dealer. He was the sole cause of the existence of the problem and its spread. Public opinion was so turned against the user, that users knew that if they did not surrender themselves for treatment, they'd be turned in by their own community. The entire nation rose as one against its common enemy—the user. It was the addict's

[1] Martin B. Margulies, "China Has No Drug Problem—Why?" *Parade*, 10/15/72. Shen Chenrv, "Keeping Narcotics Under Strict Control: Some Effects in China," *Impact on Science and Society*, No. 133, 1984. Albert P. Blaustein, ed., *Fundamental Legal Documents of Communist China* (South Hackensack, New Jersey: Fred R. Rothman and Co., 1962).

responsibility to his society to rehabilitate himself, and society's responsibility to insure that he remained rehabilitated.

Within a year most of the nation's addicts had either turned themselves in for government-sponsored treatment, rehabilitated themselves, or had gone for private treatment. Once an addict was detoxified and released, he was closely monitored by his family and community. If he relapsed, he was immediately returned to a treatment facility. In short, the demand for drugs was removed from the streets of China, and without a demand there was soon no problem of halting supply.

By spring 1951—less than two years after the beginning of the antinarcotics campaign—the New China News Agency (voice of Communist China) was able to announce that China's drug problem had been "fundamentally eradicated."

Japan[1]

The Japanese drug problem was at its height in 1963 when they followed the Chinese example and passed a strong drug law that included the mandatory commitment of drug users to mental hospitals and the registration of all drug abusers with the government. This was also accompanied by a Chinese-style propaganda campaign vilifying drug abusers and making it the duty of each citizen to aid in weeding them out. Each community had a designated leader

---

[1] "How Japan Solved Its Drug Problem," *Reader's Digest,* June 1973. Condensed from *Time,* 6/19/72. Masamutsu Naghama, "A Review of Drug Abuse and Countermeasures in Japan since World War II," *Bulletin in Narcotics,* Vol. XX, No. 3, July–September 1968. Prof. Hiroshi Kumàgai, "Drug Abuse and Countermeasures in Japan," *Medical Journal, Malaysia,* December 1974.

who was responsible for the identification and hospitalization of the addict, and later for his rehabilitation. Nine hundred hospitals were designated as addict treatment centers.

From 1963 to 1966 there was an eighty-nine-percent decline in the number of drug addicts. In a study of Japan's successful antidrug campaign Masamutsu Nagahama, chief of the Narcotics Section, Ministry of Health and Welfare, Japanese government, said, "In conclusion, we think we can state that the drug problem is under control *thanks to the strong line taken to eradicate addiction (not supply). . . .*"

Both countries were successful in their respective drug wars for two principal reasons. First, China and Japan each realized that they did not have a *drug* epidemic; they had epidemics of *druggies.* Druggies were looked upon as the cause of the problem, not the end result. They had to be isolated from the rest of the population because it was they who spread the disease—not the sellers. Second, both countries were able to involve their entire populations in community actions against drug users. It was a clear-cut case of *Together we stand, divided we fall.* The task of convincing the druggie to mend his ways was the concern not only of government but of every citizen.

Each nation's "cure" was based on the premise that once you effectively isolated the demand for drugs (druggies), supply (dealers) would quickly disappear—"demand reduction" in its purest form. Druggies were not *"offered"* drug programs or "treatment on demand," they were *"ordered"* into hospitals.

Penalties for noncompliance were swift, severe, and certain. The penalty for dealing was equally swift and certain, and often draconian. In China thirty-seven dealers were executed. Japan executed no one, but with its quickly shrinking druggie market, they didn't have to—being a drug dealer simply wasn't worth the risk. The Chinese and Japanese druggies were given exactly what their American counterparts are constantly clamoring for—treatment on demand. The only difference was that treatment was mandatory; it was based on the demand of society, not that of the druggie. Both countries recognized that the druggie is incapable of being responsible for his own actions, not to mention his own cure.

Had the Chinese and Japanese considered their druggies "victims" of "the availability of drugs" or of "the dealers," or as being "hit by a drug problem"—as our politicians and bureaucrats love to say—they would now have more drug addicts than the United States has population. Instead, they have no problem.

Whenever I think about what the United States might be like today had we instituted a program of mandatory treatment for drug users thirty years ago, instead of our phony no-win war on drugs, my first thought is of my brother David, who—after going through five rehabilitation programs, on his own volition—finally committed suicide. I am sure he, and hundreds of thousands like him, would be alive today. I also think of the hundreds of billions of wasted dollars, and all the social programs and medical research that money might have paid for.

It's time this madness stopped.

Why has the Chinese and Japanese approach never been explored in our country? The principal reason given by many experts is that the United States is a "nation of individuals" not capable of the kinds of group actions carried out by Japan and China.[1]

[1] Martin B. Margulies, "China Has No Drug Problem—Why?" *Parade*, 10/15/72.

The other reason is the three decades during which our suits, politicians, and experts have brainwashed us into accepting our drug problem as though the substance itself— cocaine, heroin, et cetera—was the enemy and the user an "innocent victim" struck down as though hit by a virus. Our problem has been described as a "disease," a "plague," and an "epidemic." Our politicians and experts have gone to great lengths convincing the American druggie that he is not morally responsible for his initial choice in using drugs —it's someone else's fault. It's the "enemy's" fault. I actually heard one addict on a television show blame his drug addiction on Manuel Noriega.[1] I even heard a top criminal trial lawyer, addressing a convention of the National Association of Trial Lawyers in Washington, D.C., say that one of the best methods of defending a drug dealer on trial was to "convince the jury that he is actually a user."[2]

It is hard to find a child in the United States who does not know that drugs are bad for him, or a human being who has been conscious for the past decade who does not know that from the moment he takes a drug he is risking becoming a ward of, and a danger to, the rest of us. The media is flooded with stories of druggie atrocities—sons who kill mothers for drug money and parents who sell their children into prostitution have become commonplace. The latest scientific studies indicate that drugs like crack and cocaine are not only violence inducing but actually destroy the parenting instinct. And yet, despite the fact that this knowledge has become hard, if not impossible, to avoid, a record number of Americans daily continue to make the conscious decision to take drugs. And still—thanks to politicians more

[1] "Anatomy of an Addict," *Geraldo Rivera Show,* NBC, May 5, 1988.
[2] Attorney Nina Ginsburg, before the National Association of Trial Lawyers, Washington, D.C., August 8, 1987.

interested in votes than lives, and experts more interested in speakers' fees and the funding of their programs than real solutions—our people are led to believe these druggies are victims.

I realize—having had a brother and daughter who were druggies—that the acceptance of the premise that the user is the enemy is a bitter pill for many of us to swallow. Often those users are our loved ones, our neighbors, even our doctors. But it is essential that we do, because it is the acceptance of this that is key to much of what follows.

THE USER—THE WEAKEST LINK

As a Drug Enforcement Administration (DEA) supervisor, working the streets of New York, I led two investigations—one an abject failure, the other a complete success. The difference between the operations: the focusing of our efforts against the druggie as opposed to the dealer. A comparison of these two cases will illustrate clearly how much easier, quicker, less costly, and less dangerous it is to eliminate drug dealers by going after their bread-and-butter: the druggie. And how this approach may be used by groups of citizens in drugproofing their communities.

Anatomy of a Failure

The 92nd Street Block Association, of the Upper West Side of Manhattan, had *had* it. The neighborhood organization, composed of middle- to upper-income business and professional people, had banded together in the common cause of trying to rescue their streets from the drug dealers. Despite their cries, complaints, and protestations to politicians, resulting in cleanup drives by the local police precinct and narcotics squads, the intersection at 92nd Street and Amsterdam Avenue had remained a "drug-dealing bazaar."

At nightfall their streets were flooded with dozens of dangerous-looking drug dealers and steerers, night phantoms who floated in and out of doorways and alleys, catering to a nonstop flow of druggie customers. The deals were made right out in the open; spotting them and making arrests was like shooting fish in a barrel. Yet, in spite of the local police cracking down periodically and making scores of dealer arrests—often arresting the same dealers two and three times —the flow continued. The police were simply outnumbered; the jails were full and the courts were turning the drug dealers loose before the arresting officers could finish their paperwork. The situation is pretty much the same in every city, town, and village in our land.

The 92nd Street Block Association was well organized and was fortunate to have among its membership some influential people with political savvy. Once they were able to demonstrate that they were not only a group of concerned citizens but a large and growing block of voters, they were able to get Congressman Charles Rangel's full attention and prompt action. The congressman, in turn, contacted the then head of the Drug Enforcement Administration, Francis "I-didn't-know-Noriega-was-in-drugs" Mullen, to demand action.[1] Within hours of the congressman's phone call to Washington, my group of twelve battle-worn DEA agents was assigned to join with the local police precinct SNEU unit in a drive *once and for all* to clean the drug dealers out of the intersection at 92nd Street and Amsterdam Avenue.

[1] Marsha Kranes, "Ex–DEA Boss: Noriega was Fair-Haired Boy," *New York Post,* 1/10/90. Mullen, the DEA Administrator from 1981 to 1985, made the statement: "I suspected [Noriega] of money laundering and selling weapons, but I still have seen nothing to indicate he was a drug trafficker."

A federal statute making it an additional crime to sell drugs within a thousand feet of a school had just been signed into law. The United States attorney for the Southern District of Manhattan, Rudolph Giuliani—himself not without political ambitions in New York City—decided that since the infamous intersection lay within a few hundred feet of a school, the dealers would also be charged with the additional crime that carried a minimum sentence of five years in prison for a first offense. It would be the first prosecution of that law in the Southern District of New York. Giuliani's office also agreed to prosecute the sales of smaller amounts of drugs than they usually accepted.[1]

And so it was with a sense of wonder that on a warm spring afternoon in 1985, twelve DEA agents teamed with twelve New York City plainclothes policemen and, with the full might and backing of the U.S. Congress and United States attorney's office, set out to drive the drug dealers from a single intersection in the heart of New York City. It was the first time I had been given so much concentrated power to work on such a small area. It turned out to be an interesting experiment.

If twelve DEA agents and a squad of police could not defeat the drug dealers of one corner in Manhattan, what hope did twenty-five hundred DEA agents have in the whole world?

The hearty souls of the 92nd Street Block Association, braving the fury of the drug dealers, allowed me to use their homes as OPs (observation posts) from where I could watch

---

[1] In 1987 the Southern District of New York rarely accepted the prosecution of drug cases involving less than a kilo of cocaine. U.S. Attorney Rudolph Giuliani, in fact, had written a memorandum to DEA requesting that "peripheral" (smaller) drug dealers not be arrested, as they would *not* be prosecuted.

drug sales and communicate what I was seeing via portable radio to my men hiding in ambush.

The situation had not been exaggerated. At darkness the intersection literally swarmed with steerers and drug dealers, fighting each other to supply an unending flow of customers who came in cars and on foot. It was a wide-open pushing-and-shoving marketplace. It was not a question of trying to catch them in the act, it was more a question of trying to guess which transaction involved the largest quantity of drugs.[1] It was indeed like shooting fish in a barrel.

Within three hours we had temporarily detained twelve drug buyers and arrested eight dealers and seized amounts of cocaine ranging from grams to a couple of ounces. Two of the dealers were armed with guns. All had been arrested and released numerous times before.

The druggies, all of whom were people with jobs and no arrest records, immediately made statements identifying the dealer they had bought from, and were—as is the custom in most courts of the United States—immediately released. *Poor victims . . .*

By midnight every single officer assigned to the operation was either tied up with paperwork, or processing and/or transporting prisoners. We would all be working for the rest of the night and long into the following day for the court hearings. Meanwhile, back at the intersection it was business as usual. The dealers were made a little more wary by the arrests, but the customers were still coming, so there was plenty of money to be made.

By morning I was still at my desk sorting out the moun-

---

[1] My instructions from the assistant United States attorney chosen to prosecute the operation were to try and develop the largest possible seizures and arrest the biggest drug dealers. User and small arrests were not popular in the media, and difficult—if not impossible—to prosecute.

tain of paperwork when the AUSA assigned to prosecute the case called. He was not too happy about being chosen to prosecute a bunch of street-level cases that neither got you headlines nor did anything for your career. Grumpily, he pointed out that most of the dealer arrests—due to the small amounts of drugs involved and because they were "jump collars" made on the basis of observations—had very little chance of standing up to the rigors of a jury trial. "God," he said, "I'd hate to go to trial with one of these dogs." The AUSA's biggest problem was that if any of the dealers didn't have enough money for bail, the Speedy Trials Act dictated that his case be brought quickly to trial—exactly what the AUSA was trying to avoid. Thus, the AUSA had refused to ask for any bail, and by nightfall, after "promising" to show up in court for an arraignment at some future date, each of the drug dealers was back on the street, none the worse for wear.

The whole effort was futile and everyone knew it—that is, everyone but the block association. They were ecstatic in the belief that *something* was finally being done. They equated action with progress, just as most of us do when we see the suits on television with another of their "biggest" drug busts, or U.S. military being dispatched to other countries to "fight" the drug war.

I gave my weary men the next twenty-four hours off and ordered them back on the street the following night. That evening, as I drove home, tired and disheartened, I detoured past the corner. It was as though we had never been there. There were more sellers on the street than the night before. Some of those we had arrested were back, fresh as daisies, looking like they'd had a good night's sleep. There were also a lot of new faces. It seemed that word of our arrests had attracted even more dealers to the corner to fill any possible gaps in supply.

A typical drug-war day was ended.

The next night, determined to make at least a couple of the arrests stick by getting evidence against a bigger dealer —a "quality case"—I decided to go undercover. I drove up to the corner in a sleek black Mercedes sedan, with a pretty, green-eyed agent from South Carolina in the backseat. As I neared the corner I hid a small tape recorder in the car's map compartment beneath my window. I announced that I was the bodyguard of a famous English rock singer and that his girlfriend was in the rear seat. "They're partying on the other side of town," I said. "The girl wants to buy a couple of ounces of coke."

We were mobbed by a dozen street-dealers and steerers who looked like they ranged from fifteen to twenty years of age, offering us breaks on price, better quality, and so on. The competition got so heated that they began fighting among themselves: *"He sells beat shit, man." "My stuff be better than his." "He a lyin' muthafucka." "I saw them first!"* et cetera, et cetera. The tape recording I have of that moment is incredible. I often play it for people who want to legalize drugs as proof that there are quite a few people in the U.S. who buy and sell drugs as though they were legal.

When it seemed that the arguing would erupt into a street fight, I chose one of the sellers who seemed the most promising (old enough to go to jail), and conned him into bringing me directly to his source by ordering what I was sure would be more cocaine than he would carry or be trusted with. There followed one of the most frightening moments of my life.

The street dealer, a Latino kid of about eighteen, brought me into an apartment full of Colombian cocaine dealers, one of the main suppliers in the neighborhood. For a moment I stood there gawking in disbelief. Right there in front of me was a large pile of white powder and a set of scales on a table. A guy with dark Indian eyes and a scraggly beard, in front of me and to my left, put his hand on a gun in his belt and watched me. Another guy moved behind me and frisked me so quickly and smoothly that in a flash I found myself unarmed and facing a drug dealer who had *my* nine-millimeter automatic in his hand. The two of us stared at each other for what seemed to me an eternity.

The idiocy of the whole thing struck me—I was about to die in this big futile lie of a drug war. The guy had nothing to lose in killing me. If he thought I was a cop, there was more than enough drugs on that table to get him a life sentence. And in New York State there is no death penalty for murder.[1]

"Hey, I'm a bodyguard," I heard myself say. For a moment everything seemed dreamlike and in slow motion. I watched my hand reaching toward the gun in his hand as though it did not belong to me and had a will of its own. I think had I hesitated a thousandth of a second too long—given him too much time to think—he would have shot me. Instead, he let me retrieve the gun, his eyes going to the others. I turned to see two other men with guns in their hands watching me. I holstered mine. Miraculously, I am still here to tell the tale. The Colombians must have believed I was nothing more than a bodyguard, but they decided not to take the chance of selling me drugs.

The Latino kid who brought me there just shrugged and said, "If they won't sell you I got another guy who will." A half hour later, three blocks away, we wound up arresting another one of the major drug suppliers in the area, seizing

---

[1] Conviction of possession of more than three ounces in New York State can mean a life sentence.

about a half pound of cocaine and a couple of guns.[1] We rushed back to try and arrest the Colombians, but found the apartment empty and as clean as if no one had ever been there.

By the end of the week, after working four twenty-four-hour shifts, all the cops and DEA agents were dragging ass. We had arrested a total of forty-seven drug dealers and seized a total of approximately a pound of cocaine and ten guns. We had also arrested more than fifty druggies (buyers) who were released after quickly confessing and tearfully identifying the dealers who had "victimized" them. In spite of the fact that possession of cocaine, in any amount, is a federal felony, not a single drug buyer was prosecuted.

Some deterrent!

By the end of the following week we had worked another three twenty-four-hour shifts and arrested an additional thirty drug dealers. Out of all the arrests only four still remained in jail and I was under heavy pressure to end the operation and get my men working on "class-one" cases.

For about three nights the corner of 92nd Street and Amsterdam Avenue remained relatively quiet with just a handful of dealers braving arrest to make a few quick sales to a few scattered customers. A check with a few local informers indicated that the "heat" had frightened a lot of buyers into looking for their drugs at other locations farther north on Amsterdam Avenue—the dealers just followed the demand. Everyone knew the change was temporary. But if you took a quick look, the street seemed quiet, so the operation was deemed a "success" and terminated. My group and I were sent back into the "real" drug war.

---

[1] Subsequent investigation revealed that this supplier was almost immediately replaced by others.

Within a week the president of the block association called me to say that all the dealers were back on the street and that it looked like business as usual. There was nothing I could do. My group was busy chasing class-one dealers and making bigger and more meaningless drug seizures, so that the suits and the politicians could hold ever more meaningless "victory" press extravaganzas. None of it would have any effect on the New York drug problem, but it *would* do wonders for careers, budgets, and elections.

I began to study the Chinese and Japanese solutions, while keeping tabs on neighborhood action groups around the country. Most had experiences similar to that of the 92nd Street Block Association. Some ended tragically in the deaths of citizens who, out of anger and frustration, tried to take on the drug dealers themselves. The killing of one woman affected me deeply. Maria Hernandez, a thirty-four-year-old mother of three, was gunned down in Brooklyn after she and her husband "fought to rid their neighborhood of drug dealers."[1]

Why should a woman, a mother of three children, be battling it out with drug dealers? Just the thought of it enraged me. Then I thought of the scores of frightened buyers we had arrested and turned loose. None of them were armed. All of them were what our society considers "casual drug users." It occurred to me that had Mrs. Hernandez and her husband confronted *them* instead of the dealers, she might be alive today and, at the same time, they might have hurt the dealers a lot more than by confronting them directly.

I also began to hear about citizens who had banded together into action groups and successfully eliminated drugs from their communities. In studying the actions taken by

[1] James C. McKinley, Jr., "Woman Who Fought Drugs," *The New York Times,* 8/9/89.

these groups, I noticed that they had inadvertently done something that both the Chinese and Japanese had done: they had created conditions so hostile for the *buying* of drugs in their communities that the druggie had to go elsewhere. The dealers would then quickly disappear. I had inadvertently done the same thing—albeit for a brief period of time—for the 92nd Street Block Association.

The dealers call it "heat." The neighborhoods were too "hot" for buyers—particularly casual users, by far the largest part of our drug market—to shop for their goodies. Of course in China and Japan there was no *elsewhere* to go to; the heat was applied on a national level.

I began to toy with the idea of conducting an experiment to see if my theory worked. I wanted to see if I could put a significant drug-dealing operation out of business without arresting a single dealer. For the experiment to be meaningful I needed a notorious drug den that had resisted all conventional law-enforcement efforts to close it down. I did not have long to wait before the perfect situation presented itself.

A SMALL EXPERIMENT WITH BIG IMPLICATIONS

On March 15, 1989, an article appeared in *The New York Times* about the Dominican cocaine and crack gangs controlling West 109th Street in Manhattan.[1] Drug dealing was so profitable in the neighborhood that as fast as the police arrested a seller, another would immediately replace him. Thousands of arrests had been made on the street, yet the

[1] Selwyn Raab, "Brutal Gangs Wage War of Terror in Upper Manhattan," *The New York Times,* 3/15/89.

drug business had never been "healthier" or more profitable.

I had a friend who lived in the ground-floor apartment of one of the most raided buildings on that street. My friend's front window faced the street above the entrance gate to two basement apartments that, in reality, were drug supermarkets specializing in cocaine and crack. According to my friend customers' cars—in spite of the basement's being raided by the local police on an almost weekly basis—would still line up throughout the night, every night, to buy drugs. It sounded like the ideal place for my experiment. I was invited to witness the action with my own eyes.

I spent about a week sitting in a darkened window watching car after car arrive, most of them with out-of-state license plates, carrying well-dressed middle- to upper-income people out to buy some "recreational drugs."

Some of the customers looked as though they might have been part of the many audiences of "concerned" parent organizations I had addressed over the years on behalf of DEA. People who would stare at me in silent guilt when I would say, "If our national drug appetite is anywhere near the reported $200 billion a year, then—if I could search all your houses right now—statistically speaking, I would *have* to find at least a half-million dollars' worth of drugs."

Once again I found myself witnessing drug transactions that were done so openly that I had to remind myself that I was watching a felony punishable under federal law by fifteen years in prison. A car would pull up and double-park, the motor left running. Either the driver or the passenger would get out and casually cross the sidewalk, skip down the basement steps below me, and knock on the window. Sometimes I could hear them say what they wanted—*an eighth, an ounce, a gram, some love drug.* Some of the buyers would have a difficult time making themselves understood by the dealers, who were mostly non–English-speaking illegal aliens from the Dominican Republic. The amounts and prices had to be repeated several times, until the conversation could be heard halfway up the street. The buyers were no more worried about police than if they had been buying stereo equipment. The door would then bang open and the buyer be admitted. Usually the transaction (the weighing of the drugs and the counting of the money) would take no longer than ten minutes.

At times there was a line of seven or eight cars double parked waiting to make a buy. Marked patrol cars would cruise by slowly, knowing exactly what was going on, but unable, legally and by police-department regulations, to do anything.[1] The buyers would glance at them with unworried eyes. The patrolmen would glare their impotent anger and continue on their way. At times an angry, frustrated cop would order a line of cars to move on. They would then have to go through all the trouble of driving around the block until he had left. It was like that every night I was there.

Even the police raids were routine, if not casual. One night, in the midst of thriving dope business, a half-dozen marked and unmarked police cars screeched to a halt out front. I could hear screaming and banging below as the drug dealers fought to flee out rear exits. The whole neighborhood poured out onto the street to watch the fun. Plainclothes officers raced headlong, guns drawn, into the basement while uniformed officers stopped people on the street.

[1] The New York City Police Department, as do many metropolitan police departments around the country, discourage uniformed divisions from making drug arrests. It takes the officers off the street for too long a period of time, and the arrests are usually jump collars that don't stand up in court.

The floor beneath my feet vibrated with shouts and banging. Within minutes the whole thing was over.

Four grinning illegal-alien drug dealers were marched out handcuffed behind their backs and stuffed into patrol cars. Each, as a symbol of his status in the drug world, was laden with gold. The cops looked weary, even bored; they had been through the drill a dozen times before. Car doors slammed, engines roared, and the dealers were on their way to pay their twenty-four-hours-in-jail dues. The processing of each dealer cost the taxpayers ten to twenty thousand dollars (depending on which politician you believe) and was for naught. It is a scene repeated across our nation tens of thousands of times each day.

The police cars were barely out of sight when four new dealers slipped into the basement. A new line of cars bearing buyers was already waiting. Within minutes it was business as usual. The city's politicians had been given their weekly sacrifice—arrest statistics had risen a point or two and there were dozens of suits and politicians ready to claim responsibility for it. *The drug war marches on.* A whole squad of police officers now had about a week's worth of paperwork. If anything, business was now somewhat *more* relaxed (if that was possible) than before the raid. Everyone knew that it would be at least a week or two before the next one. My friend assured me that it had been like that for the past two years.

The location was perfect for my experiment. But before I could put it into action I had to get authorization from DEA and a prosecutor,[1] and that wasn't going to be easy. By focusing the resources of my enforcement group against the user instead of the dealer, I would be operating in direct contradiction to the Big Lie.

[1] A requirement for beginning any DEA investigation.

The true purpose of the operation, which I secretly dubbed "Operation True Demand Reduction," had to be kept secret from both the DEA suits and the United States attorney's office. The head of DEA's New York office (a media-conscious man whose love of seeing himself on the little screen earned him the nickname "Captain Video"), knew that arresting users and low-level street dealers was not the way to attract the attention of the press. Rudolph Giuliani, the United States attorney for the Southern District of New York, himself a media and politically minded man (as are most U. S. attorneys), had instituted a policy against prosecuting "peripheral" (smaller) drug dealers. Users were never prosecuted. Prosecution was rarely authorized for arrests involving less than a kilo of cocaine—a greater quantity than any street-level dealer would ever handle. Thus, getting approval for an enforcement operation that would focus on the user was going to be no easy matter.

I first approached my division leader about beginning the 109th Street operation with the pretext that I needed to work a low-level street operation to give some of the rookies in my group street experience (three brand-new agents had just been transferred into the group, fresh out of the academy). Like young birds of prey they had to get their first taste of blood. I said that I wanted them to experience how to manage a drug case, from the street arrest, to the flipping of the defendant and the obtaining of enough PC (probable cause) for a search-and-arrest warrant, to the final raid. And there was no better way to begin than arresting the buyers at the 109th street basement. I used *The New York Times* article to bolster my case that what we were ultimately after were "major dealers."

The idea of arresting buyers was not a comfortable one for an assistant special agent in charge (ASAC). He had been an experienced street agent himself (rare for anyone at his level) and suspected that I had something up my sleeve, but gave the okay anyway. "Don't overdo it," he warned. "You know what Captain Video thinks of street cases."

The next step was finding a prosecutor who would authorize the arrests. I knew I would have no chance getting authorization from Giuliani's office, so I contacted Sterling Johnson, New York City's special narcotics prosecutor. I had known Sterling a long time and did not have to con him. He was one of the few people with political clout who was sincere about wanting to win a drug war; and a gambler unafraid of sacrificing good press for a principle—a rare combination. He loved the idea and immediately authorized the case. With the courts as clogged as they were he could not guarantee that the buyers would be prosecuted, but at least I had the authorization to make the arrests. Operation True Demand Reduction was in business.

The first night I positioned four radio cars with two agents in each at the far end of 109th Street, where the druggies had to pass after making their buys. I sat at the window of the darkened apartment with a portable radio in my hand. Once again, it was like shooting fish in a barrel. By three A.M. we had grabbed eight yuppies, a couple of grams of coke and crack, and three cars. All of them flipped, crying and blubbering about their careers and their families, and signed full confessions and statements describing the sellers and agreeing to testify in any court, or anything else we wanted, if I would only let them go.

"I don't know why I ever got started," cried a New Jersey white-collar worker. "God, if my family finds out . . . Please let me go. I swear I'll never do it again." I wasn't too sure about the *never,* but I *was* sure it would never again be on 109th street. And that was good enough for my experiment.

All the poor "victimized" users were arrested and made to spend the night in jail with people they would not have dreamed of being alone with on a public beach, not to mention locked up in the same cage with. It would be a long time before any of them would recover from the experience. And more importantly—now that it was clear that the location they had bought drugs at was "hot"—each would warn everyone he knew to stay away. I already had more than enough descriptions and signed statements to arrest the people in the basement, but that would have just been the history of the past two years repeating itself. The place would be open for business as soon as we left with our prisoners. I wanted to see what would happen if we kept locking up the buyers and the word that the location was a bad one to buy drugs in kept spreading.

Over the next week, from March 24 to March 29, night after night, group 22 kept locking up buyers. Most of them flipped, signed statements, and blubbered that they would never do it again. One young retail-store manager said he was "glad" he had been caught. The one thing that seemed apparent to me was that most of them never would have been buying drugs in the first place if they'd anything to fear from the law.

By the end of the week we had arrest and search warrants for the dealers and the basement. The flow of buyers had diminished to a trickle. In the meantime the small, "insignificant" arrests were causing an uproar among the ADAs who had to process them. I was put under increasing pressure to end the operation. My division leader warned me that Captain Video had made a point of criticizing me for the large volume of small arrests my group had been making lately. I finally succumbed and planned the raids for March 30, the next night. It would be our last night of terrorizing the drug buyers of 109th Street.

A strange thing happened on the night of the twenty-ninth. I had ten agents in five cars hidden within a three-block radius of the basement. All of them were watching street sales going on around them like it was going out of style, but not a customer had arrived at the basement apartments. Around midnight I saw one of the rarest sights ever seen in the streets of New York—drug dealers and no buyers. Two of the dealers came out of the basement and stood on the street looking up and down the block for a few moments. *"Qué pasa?* (What's happening?)" said one. The other looked around and shrugged his shoulders, *"Quién sabe?* (Who knows?)"

On the evening of March 30 we raided the basement and found it empty. They had closed down operations. For the first time in two years, after scores of police raids, the drug den had been closed down. We had successfully closed it down by attacking its life's blood—the druggie. And it wasn't all that hard, and a lot less dangerous than going to war against the dealers.

Of course, the dealers had probably moved to another location with less heat and were still selling. But what would happen if our national policy were changed to attack the user as the enemy, and there were no such thing as a location with less heat? China and Japan did it, why not America?

And most important, the immediate improvement in the quality of life for the people living in and around this particular building was remarkable. No more cars were lined up blowing their horns all night. No more fears of a gunfight breaking out over a bad drug deal. No more flow of druggies in and out of their building, stepping over their playing children. A hundred-percent reduction of sleaze in their lives. Drugs were still all over the neighborhood, but for this

one small group of hardened New Yorkers, life was better
. . . much better.

What might have happened if I had enough men, resources, and support to conduct the experiment to include
the whole block, the whole neighborhood, or a whole town
somewhere? I was excited by the possibilities, but kept my
mouth shut. To the DEA suits it was just another case that
had turned out badly.

I spoke to Sterling Johnson about teaming my group with
some city cops to broaden the experiment to one of the
worst crack-selling blocks in Washington Heights. He liked
the idea. The big problem would be "selling" the idea to
Captain Video. I figured that I would present him with a
plan that would enable him to appear before the media as a
"pioneer" in drug enforcement. *Screw the credit! Let the
suits have it.* I just wanted to see something change during
my career. I had started out almost a quarter of a century
before, believing I'd have an effect; now maybe I would.

*The plan would never be attempted. Two months later I
was injured during a crack raid in Washington Heights and
would be out of action until my retirement nine months later.*

Over the next two months I drove through 109th Street
often to see if the dealers had returned to that basement.
They never did. I am not claiming that they never will, or
that I had cleaned up the neighborhood. Quite the contrary,
drugs were still being sold both openly and in great quantity
on both ends of the block. But it was gratifying to me to see
the difference in life-style for the people in *those* two buildings mirrored on their smiling faces as they sat on stoops
they had spent years fearing to walk across; or looking out
of windows that used to remain closed and locked on the
hottest of summer days. Then I began to wonder what
would happen to them when some new drug dealer with a

new flock of customers decided to take up residence in the basement apartments again. What could these people do?

Plenty!

All my group of twelve agents did was to make that particular location too hot for drug buyers. We had pitted ourselves against ordinary, unarmed citizens who saw nothing wrong in buying some "recreational" drugs in someone else's neighborhood—the kind of drug consumer that accounts for the fattest portion of our $200-billion-a-year drug habit. If we could eliminate this "soft consumer" and the huge portion of the drug market he represents, we would be cutting our nation's drug demand back by tens of billions of dollars; and we would *really* be taking the profit out of drug dealing. Once the soft market was gone, the remaining drug dealers would be the easy problem for law enforcement that they had been, prior to the popularization of "recreational drugs."

The beauty of destroying the drug dealer by cutting off his fattest source of income, is that it's something that *any* group of citizens can do in their community, town, or village, and not a single gun or badge is necessary.

2

Organizing Against the User

Once you have accepted the fact that the only enemy to be defeated in this war is the drug consumer, the next step in ridding your community of his presence is to organize against him and him alone. He is the weakest link, the easiest to defeat, and the least dangerous.

Right from the outset it should be made clear to all members and prospective members of your neighborhood organization that the ONLY reason for its existence is the elimination of druggies from your town, village, block, or building —whatever your group designates as its living space. Conversely, it must also be understood that the organization is NEVER, UNDER ANY CIRCUMSTANCES, TO TAKE ACTION AGAINST DRUG DEALERS. They are too dangerous and— thanks to the druggie—too well financed. Law-enforcement agencies have not been able to control them in thirty years; a neighborhood organization made up of civilians won't have a chance.

NAMING THE ORGANIZATION
(The BAD Organization)

The word *bad* in street jargon can also mean something "mean," or "tough," and usually refers to something that is exceptionally "good." I think it a perfect acronym for an organization of citizens who are fed up with talk and are ready ". . . to do all that is necessary *within the law* to Banish All Druggies from their living space." I believe that beginning with the choice of the organization's name the community's attitude should be clearly and unequivocally expressed. Whether you choose the name BAD Organization or not is unimportant. What *is* important is that the name be indicative of a group formed, organized, equipped, and educated with only one primary goal in mind—making your neighborhood a BAD one for the BUYING of drugs.

A BAD organization is *not* a social or philanthropic organization. It *is* an action-oriented group ready to make its presence felt in the streets, schools, courts, media, and political world, in taking whatever *legal* action is necessary to keep druggies out of its community.

RECRUITING AND ORGANIZING

All citizens of your community should be contacted for their membership and support. If the latest polls indicating how fed up our society is with drugs are anywhere near correct—with a majority of Americans ready to surrender civil rights to win a drug war—getting your community's cooperation should be no problem. A particular effort should be made to recruit members of law enforcement and the legal professions living in your community. Their advice and counsel will be important and the fact that they, too, are members of the community gives them a personal stake in the organization's success.

AN EMPHASIS ON YOUTH

(An Alternative to Drug Abuse)

A heavy emphasis should be placed on including the community's youth in the organization. Exposing them to the strong antidruggie sentiment, and perhaps giving them an opportunity to form their own auxiliary youth group, with a tough, cool, no-nonsense image such as the Guardian Angels have, will be a powerful weapon against peer pressure. The druggie in the community is the one who should be made to feel the "chicken," too cowardly to face life without chemicals—a "punk," a "jerk," an "outsider."

CODIFY THE ORGANIZATION'S PURPOSE FOR EXISTING

Once formed, the BAD organization's one and only goal and purpose for existing should be codified in some manner, with individuals and committees being given the responsibility for insuring that the group is trained and equipped and that its each and every activity is planned and executed with that one goal in mind.

Too many organizations I have known—that began with the broad intention of "fighting drugs"—quickly became nothing more than social clubs where neighbors could meet monthly for coffee and donuts with the local suits and politicians who would listen with professional sympathy to their gripes, while the druggies and dealers scuttled all over their streets, buildings, and rooftops. To avoid this fate I recommend the strict adherence to a Declaration of Purpose that will keep your group on track. An example of one might be as follows:

DECLARATION OF PURPOSE
(Your community) BAD ORGANIZATION

The main purpose of our existence is to create in (your community) the most hostile environment possible for the DRUG CONSUMER. To this end we will take direct action—always operating within the limits of the law—in the following areas:

1. NEIGHBORHOOD. We will create an atmosphere on the streets or our (town, village, community, housing development, et cetera) that is as hostile and adverse as possible for the *drug consumer.*

2. CRIMINAL JUSTICE SYSTEM. We will—by vigilance in the court systems, political action and influence, and liaison with the media—do all that is possible to insure that all DRUGGIE (drug consumer) arrests on our streets are prosecuted to the extreme limits of the law.

3. MEDIA. We will, by all the means at our command, see that *all* arrests of druggies are well publicized; and that the actions of law-enforcement officials, politicians, and judges that are contrary to our goal are also well publicized.

4. POLITICAL. We will insure that *all* members of our community are registered to vote, and do all that is possible—within the limits of the law—to insure that the community votes for and supports *only* those candidates for public office who support the goals and philosophies of the community organization. We will also seek and support all forms of legislation aimed at making the law a deterrent to DRUG ABUSE (e.g., drug testing; druggies' loss of driving privileges; making preg-

nant druggie mothers responsible for damages to unborn fetuses, and so on).

5. LAW ENFORCEMENT.

a. We will take all actions possible to convince law-enforcement authorities to direct the majority of their resources at combating the DRUG CONSUMERS in (your neighborhood)—as opposed to DRUG DEALERS.

b. We will at no time take direct actions against DRUG DEALERS, other than to assist the efforts of law-enforcement authorities.

c. We will at no time violate any laws (federal, state, or city) in the attainment of our goals.

d. We will maintain a full-time liaison with federal, state, and local law-enforcement authorities to insure that we are not working at cross-purposes, and to gain their full support in the attainment of our goals.

6. LIAISON WITH OTHER CITIZENS' GROUPS. We will maintain liaison and enter into mutual-support agreements with any other organization of citizens with goals and bylaws similar to ours.

7. LIAISON WITH THE BUSINESS COMMUNITY. We will maintain full-time liaison with our business community in the spirit of mutual support in ridding our community of druggies.

8. SCHOOLS. We will maintain an active participation in our childrens' education and an aggressive vigilance over our community's schools, to insure that our children are educated in a DRUGGIE-free environment.

9. YOUTH. We will make a special effort at including and emphasizing the participation of our community's youth in all our activities.

EQUIPMENT

The following is some of the equipment, already in use by several successful citizens' groups around the country, which I recommend that all community antidrug groups have at their disposal:

1. Bullhorns and loudspeakers.

2. Radio communications. CB radio systems are now available at reasonable prices. A base, or monitoring station, should be placed with your local police, if possible.

3. Conventional and video camera equipment with tele-photo- and night-lens capability.

4. Handcuffs, nightsticks, and other police equipment for possible use in citizen's-arrest situations. (Not to be done without prior training and legal advice.)

5. Armbands, identifying jackets, or other "uniform" clearly identifying your group to law enforcement and drug-gie alike. The uniform should be representative of the organization's pride in itself and the seriousness of its intent.

6. Several used cars and/or vans equipped with CB radios and/or telephones, and—if feasible—loudspeaker equipment. The vehicles are to be plainly marked with the organization's name and logo.

SOURCES OF OUTSIDE FINANCIAL SUPPORT

The Business Community

After having spoken to hundreds of businessmen and merchants, desperate for any action to rid their neighbor-hoods of drugs, I doubt that a well-organized community will have any difficulty in getting most of its equipment in the form of donations.

Federal, State, and Local Grants

The good news is that some of our honest and well-meaning politicians are finally seeing the light and recognizing that the key to winning a drug war is the huge, untapped source of energy and power represented by our nation's action-oriented citizens' organizations. The federal government and many states, cities, and local governments are offering grants to well-organized community antidrug organizations.

The bad news is that many of the people with their fingers on the purse strings are still mired in the get-the-dealer, Big Lie philosophy that, hopefully, will soon change. A perfect example of this was found in the statement of Health and Human Services Secretary Louis W. Sullivan, during his White House announcement of grants of $42 million to ninety-five coalitions of community groups. "Those who deal in community spirit will win [the drug war]," he said. "Let the *traffickers and drug dealers* take note of what we do here today. They may fear the police, but they should fear an angry and active community even more."[1] What a shame. Mr. Sullivan was only half correct. Had he said, "Let the *drug users* take note of what we do here . . ." this drug war would have been close to over.

TRAINING AND EDUCATION

Do not be alarmed by my educational recommendations, which will appear a lot more formal and complicated than

[1] Carolyn Skorneck, "Drug Prevention," AP news release, 10/4/90.

they are in reality. I think a week of training and discussion, as a group, will be sufficient before taking action. What must be kept in mind is that *the group is not intended to act as a police agency.* Rather, it will be *the visible and vocal expression of the community's outrage at the presence of drug consumers in its environment.*

The primary sources of training and expertise should be your local police, federal and state district attorney's offices, and colleges and universities. Another important source of training and expertise are the small but growing number of *successful* neighborhood organizations and citizen action groups around the country such as the Guardian Angels. If the proper liaison and groundwork has been done, there should be no lack of training expertise available to your group.

Training should cover the following subjects:

1. *Probable cause:* How to recognize drug-trafficking activity, with particular emphasis on when there is legal *probable cause* to believe that a **drug buyer** has purchased and is carrying drugs.

2. *Citizen's arrest powers:* Under what conditions you, as a private citizen, can stop, search, detain, and restrain until the police come and arrest a **drug buyer** in possession of drugs. These powers differ from place to place and have to be approached according to where your organization is located.

3. *The drug business:* The "business" of dealing drugs is all around us to the tune of almost $200 billion a year, affecting virtually every phase of our daily lives. We must learn as much as we can about the business, with a particular emphasis on how it affects our target—DRUG BUYERS.

a. Common drugs of abuse and their effects, particularly those found in your living environment. Crack and cocaine are now the drugs of choice and should be the ones that concern most organizations. (See Appendix I.)

b. Familiarization with appearance, packaging, and pharmacology of drugs of frequent abuse. (See Appendix I.)

c. Jargon or terminology used in the drug business, both by law enforcement and druggies. (See Glossary.)

d. Drug-trafficking patterns in your community.

4. *Technical equipment:* The group should thoroughly familiarize itself with the following equipment:

a. CB radio equipment. Base stations and mobile car equipment. Any reputable radio equipment and/or car dealer will be more than happy to furnish full instruction and installation.

b. Loudspeakers and bullhorns.

c. Camera and video equipment. The best source of training is a reputable dealer, or a police surveillance expert. The use of this equipment is surprisingly simple and I've rarely found a group of people among whom there weren't several with a special aptitude toward it.

d. Automobiles and other motor vehicles to be used for citizen patrols. Guidelines should be arranged with local law enforcement. REMEMBER—YOU ARE TO OBEY ALL TRAFFIC LAWS AND *NEVER* TO ENGAGE IN PURSUIT DRIVING. Such tactics in the confrontation with drug consumers should never become necessary. (See chapter 3, Antidruggie Tactics.)

Hopefully, the education of Americans in the nuts-and-bolts basics of the daily drug economy will have a significant overall effect on our government's sham drug war. In my long experience of addressing audiences, first as a speaker for DEA and then, after my retirement, as a writer and lecturer, I have been astounded at how little people know about the realities of a problem that has so affected their lives.

LIAISON WITH LAW ENFORCEMENT AND POLITICIANS, AND RESISTANCE

(Combating the Big Lie)

As one of its primary goals the BAD organization should do everything possible to pressure local law enforcement and politicians to focus most of their resources against the drug consumer. For instance, if it were publicized in the media that all police activity in a certain area was to be devoted heavily—if not exclusively—to the arrest and prosecution of *drug buyers,* an immediate and marked improvement in the drug-trafficking patterns would occur. This has been the experience of the TNT program (see Glossary) in New York City and of other similar programs around the country.

Such measures, however, are considered "emergency" and "stopgap," and are unpopular with the suits and politicians because, while their effectiveness is dramatic, they are not headline grabbers.[1] And our politicians, most of whom have spent three decades convincing the American people that the druggie is a victim, now fear telling them the truth —that the druggie, many of whom are the loved ones of voters, is the enemy. Unfortunately for us, there are too

---

[1] At this writing—in spite of the drug problem being reduced to almost nonexistent in every neighborhood where TNT action had been instituted —New York City is considering ending the program because large numbers of arrests and large media-grabbing seizures are no longer being made.

many politicians more interested in winning elections than in winning a drug war.

A look at almost any American newspaper on any day will verify that our law-enforcement officials and politicians are solidly entrenched in the "get-the-dealer" and the "biggest-drug-seizure-ever" philosophy of fighting the drug war —the Big Lie. They know that their images on television screens and on the front pages of newspapers, standing before tables piled high with drugs announcing another "major drug war victory," is going to convince you to vote for them and fund their ever-growing bureaucracies. Unfortunately, for the past three decades they have been right. So when you approach them with the request that law-enforcement efforts in your community be focused on the drug buyer, you are going to meet great resistance; don't be discouraged by it—expect it!

Your group should at no time be at odds with law enforcement; there should be a pledge of mutual support. Inform your local police that your goal is to make your neighborhood one that DRUG CONSUMERS would rather avoid, and that to this end you would like their advice, support, training, and as much active participation with your group as they can afford.

Once you've convinced local politicians of your voting power, there should be no problem in garnering at least the cooperation of law enforcement. Just as the 92nd Street Block Association was able to influence a congressman into pressuring the New York City police and the DEA into a concerted, albeit failed, attack on the corner drug dealers, your organization can do the same. Only, this time the weapons will be aimed at the right target.

RALLYING CRY

Any attempt to take meaningful action against drug users can be expected to meet with resistance from the law-enforcement, rehabilitation, and political sectors—each has its own jealously guarded vested interest in the drug wars. However, the thing to remember is that for three decades, none of these sectors has been able to prove its effectiveness. Despite all their efforts, alleged expertise, and the expenditure of hundreds of billions of our tax dollars, our drug problem—as measured by drug consumption; the deteriorating quality of our lives; drug-related violence, death, and crime—is worse than ever. And throughout these three decades of failed drug war, the enormous energy and resources of American business and citizens' organizations have been either untapped or misused.

We Americans have been conned into standing on the sidelines of the so-called war on drugs, rooting for a "win" that will never come; while our business community is duped, year after year, to contribute to treatment, prevention, and education programs that range from ineffective to criminal rip-offs. It is time for a change in approach; a time for Americans to roll up their sleeves and get personally involved and stop leaving the problem to the "experts"; a time to attack the drug problem with methods that have already been proven effective; a time for the immense power of the will of the American people to be harnessed and aimed at the weakest link. A BAD organization's rallying cry should be:

Say, "Get lost!" to druggies.

3

Antidruggie Tactics

(Urban and Inner-City Areas)

Important to note: many antidruggie techniques, tactics, and strategies recommended for urban areas may be useful in certain suburban and rural situations as well, and vice versa. In order to get the full benefit of the information in these pages—no matter what type of community you live in—this book should be read in its entirety. Also, before engaging in any of the tactics or techniques discussed in this book, citizens groups should obtain instruction and guidance from their local police and prosecutors' offices as to the use of any particular tactic or technique in their neighborhoods.

CREATING A BAD NEIGHBORHOOD FOR DRUG SHOPPING

If three decades of trying to win the drug war by attacking supply has taught us anything, it is that the threat of arrest, long prison sentences, and even death has no effect in convincing drug dealers to take up another vocation; there is simply too much money to be made. As the 109th Street experiment showed, even regular police raids are ineffective. As long as there are druggies with cash, there will always be sellers to supply them.

On the other hand we have also learned that it does not take much to frighten the druggie into changing his buying habits. Especially when the vast majority of drug buyers make up the "soft market"—the so-called "straight" people with jobs, families, and reputations to protect. The latest statistics indicate that most illegal drug consumers are people who earn more than $50,000 a year.[1] These "responsible" citizens, who convince themselves that they are doing no harm by a little "recreational drug" use, are the easiest to frighten into changing their entertainment habits. Even the hardest hard-core, garbage-head druggie will avoid an area where he has the slightest suspicion he will have a hassle in copping drugs.

And that is precisely what this section is going to concentrate on—making your community a frightening place for drug buyers; a place they will want to avoid like a Pia Zadora film festival. Creating such a community is easily accomplished through three types of strategies: **The Visible Threat, Tactical Street Action,** and **Strategic Action.**

THE VISIBLE THREAT

It bears repeating (and to keep repeating) that the only goal of the BAD organization is to make the *buying* of drugs in its community a difficult, if not a terrifying, experience. One of the inherent weaknesses of being a druggie— particularly one of the eighty percent whose drug of preference is cocaine or crack—is that the drugs themselves induce an overpowering feeling of paranoia. It is precisely this feeling that we are going to exploit to the hilt.

The first line of defense against a druggie entering your living space to make a buy is the creation of an atmosphere that is as visibly threatening as possible. From the moment he enters *your* neighborhood his cold, self-centered little heart should be beating double time. He should SEE plenty

[1] Article by Richard L. Berke, *The New York Times,* 9/12/89 Page B8.

of indications that if he doesn't just scurry his sorry butt over to another neighborhood to numb his brain, he is going to face a lot of hassles, exposure, and the possibility of arrest. He should feel overwhelmed by *visible evidence* of the community's anger and intolerance of his presence. My twenty-five years of experience tells me that an effective **Visible Threat** zone will be enough to persuade even the most hardened, degenerate druggies to look for a safer place to do their shopping.

An Example of the Effectiveness of the Visible Threat

Last year a friend of mine, Joe,[1] the owner of a restaurant on world famous Restaurant Row in New York City's theater district, called me as a last resort. He and his fellow restaurant owners were desperate. Crack and cocaine dealers had taken over the street. Their businesses were being destroyed. Joe and the other owners had called the local suits and politicians, which resulted in more sporadic dealer arrests, which in turn—as happened on 109th Street—had no effect on the problem whatsoever.

"Well, what the hell are we supposed to do?" asked Joe. "These bastards are really hurting us. People come from out of town and they've got to run a gauntlet of drug deals to get to the restaurant. They'd rather go back to their hotels and eat, and I can't blame them." He threw his arms up in frustration. "First the stock-market crash in October, and now this."

I really wanted to help Joe. We had met almost ten years earlier when he had been working as a bartender in a place where I was doing some undercover work. Joe—thanks to

[1] Name changed for his protection.

the drunken babbling of the girlfriend of another agent—
had learned that I was a narc. He had everything to lose and
nothing to gain by protecting my identity. Some of his customers were bad dudes who, if they had the slightest suspicion that he'd known who I was, would have killed him
without blinking an eye. But Joe had kept his mouth shut
and never even hinted to me that he knew who I was.

It was not until six years later, after I had returned from
working overseas and Joe had called DEA's New York office looking for me, that I learned how he had protected me.
During the intervening years he had worked hard, saved his
money, begged, borrowed, and mortgaged everything he
had to become the owner of one of New York's prime res-
taurants. It was the American dream come true, only it was
about to be destroyed by the American nightmare. I didn't
have the heart to tell him how badly the deck was stacked
against him; and how little the suits and politicians really
cared about his plight, or anyone else's for that matter, except for those with political clout.

"Let me check it out myself," I said. "I can't promise you
anything, but I'll see." If there was anything I could do for
the guy, I was determined to do it. What I had in mind was
another, somewhat more expanded, 109th Street experiment.

Three of my men and I cruised the area in undercover
cars. We didn't have to look very far for dealers. When I
stopped for a light at the corner of Seventh Avenue and
Restaurant Row, a dealer knocked on the window of my
Mercedes 300 SL and tried to sell me some crack. He heard
the crackle of my government radio and grinned knowingly.
He turned and nonchalantly stepped back on the curb to
join a group of a half dozen just like him. He said something
to the others and they all turned to leer defiantly at me until
the light turned green. I continued past the corner watching

them in my rearview mirror. The dealer saluted me with his middle finger high in the air.

The law really frightens these guys.

As well as being numerous, the dealers were spread out along the whole length of the long block, from Eighth to Seventh Avenue, supplying a steady flow of customers, ninety-nine percent of whom seemed to be clean-cut teenagers, yuppies, and blue- and white-collar workers—straight society.

The street was an open-air drug market. There was no way I would be able to mount a druggie harassment operation in an area that size with a twelve-man group. Four or five arrests and my whole group would be off the street doing paperwork for the next forty-eight hours. We could have arrested as many dealers as we wanted. But from the number of cash customers on the street, no number of arrests would have made a difference.

"So what the hell am I supposed to do?" Joe threw his hands up in frustration. "Go out of business?"

"No," I said. "I'm going to recommend that you do something, but I don't want you to tell anyone that it came from me."

"Look Mike, I'm ready to make a deal with the devil."

"Get hold of the Guardian Angels," I heard myself say, naming the youthful red-beret-wearing organization that the suits love to describe as "vigilantes"—the same suits who hate to acknowledge that the group wouldn't exist if law enforcement were able to do its job.

"The cops can't do anything," said Joe. "You think the Angels can?"

"They're private citizens without pensions or politics to worry about," I said. "The drug buyers know that the cops aren't going to bust them; but they can't be sure *what* the Angels will do."

What I was counting on was the **visible threat** of the uniformed, aggressive young men and women, who saw no difference between dealer and buyer. I believed it would frighten the druggies out of the area. The dealers would have no alternative but to follow.

The owners' association contacted the Guardian Angels and what happened next is history. Over the next several weeks the owners not only received the full benefit of the **visible threat** presented by the no-nonsense visage of squads of grim-faced, martial-arts-trained Guardian Angels, but also the advantage of some heavy news coverage. The media was filled with stories of the Angels patrolling Restaurant Row. In spite of statements made by suits, politicians, and bureaucrats against their use, the restaurant owners stuck to their guns and would not be dissuaded. Restaurant Row suddenly became a BAD place to buy drugs—too much of a hassle for the very sensitive, very paranoid druggie. It was much easier for them to shop elsewhere. The operation—for as long as the Angels stayed—was an unqualified success.

An almost tragic incident occurred that highlighted the dangerous difference between confronting dealers as op-posed to druggies. As visible and imposing a threat as the presence of the Guardian Angels was, it did not impress or frighten the drug dealers in the least. One heroic young Angel tried to make a citizen's arrest of a dealer and was stabbed, the blade coming within a hair of his heart. Thank God he lived. There aren't enough brave young men of con-science to go around in this world. But the lesson bears repeating: Members of a BAD organization are NEVER to confront drug dealers. Leave them to the police.

THE CREATION OF A VISIBLE THREAT

Consider your neighborhood as though it were a corn field, and the visible threats recommended here a series of scarecrows. The suggestions that follow may be used, improved upon, or disregarded and replaced with ideas of your own. The only limitation is your own imagination.

1. *Metal signs* should be posted throughout the neighborhood indicating that BUYING drugs is going to be a very risky business.

a. The signs should be large, plentiful, and posted in difficult-to-reach but very visible locations such as the sheer sides of buildings and on telephone and utility poles. And if large billboards are available, use them.

b. The signs should be floodlit so that they appear as an angry glare at night.

c. They should be as *angry* and *intimidating* as possible, giving the druggie the uncomfortable feeling of being in a hostile place where people are outraged by his presence. For example, you might put a large billboard sign on the sheer wall of a building along a street entering your community that reads:

WARNING TO DRUG BUYERS!
THIS IS A BAD NEIGHBORHOOD TO BUY YOUR STUFF! ALL DRUG TRANSACTIONS ARE BEING FILMED BY HIDDEN CAMERAS. WE WILL PRESS CHARGES AND DO ALL THAT IS POSSIBLE TO SEE THAT DRUG BUYERS RECEIVE THE MAXIMUM PENALTY ALLOWED BY LAW.

BE SMART, OR BE SORRY! TAKE YOUR DRUG MONEY AND SHOP ELSEWHERE!

This sign posted by citizens committee to Ban All Druggies
(BAD).

2. *Similar signs* should also be posted in the entrances,
hallways, and elevators of multidwelling buildings being
used by drug dealers. An example of this type of sign is:

DRUG BUYERS BEWARE!
CAMERAS ARE FILMING ALL STRANGERS
ENTERING THIS BUILDING. THESE WILL BE
TURNED OVER TO THE POLICE, THE DRUG
ENFORCEMENT ADMINISTRATION, AND THE
FEDERAL BUREAU OF INVESTIGATION.

This sign posted by (your neighborhood/building)
BAD—Banish All Druggies—committee.

Take it from a veteran of twenty-five years of narcotics
enforcement, a sign like this one, posted on any building,
along with a well-protected video camera, will do more
good cleaning out that particular building than a weekly
drug raid.

By now you get the point—the type, size, and content of
your signs and other visible threats are restricted only by
your creativity. What must be remembered is that most
drug buyers are either "straight" people with jobs and families who are already paranoid about exposure and arrest, or
drug-using criminals on probation or parole for other
crimes and equally terrified of being exposed and caught.
Their mentality is totally contrary to that of drug dealers,
who factor in arrest as part of the cost of doing a very
lucrative business.

3. *Bright lights* represent a Visible Threat to druggie and
dealer alike, and should be installed throughout a drug-traf-

ficking area—the brighter the better. Every effort must be made to insure that they are kept in repair. It is important enough that the group should designate a committee whose main function is the maintenance of the neighborhood's lighting. At night both dealers and buyers will avoid well-lighted streets like the plague. My experience tells me that there are many landlords in drug-blighted areas, who—were there a citizens' group they could count on—would gladly install floodlights on the walls of their buildings.

a. Floodlights should be placed high up on the walls of apartment buildings or utility poles, so that they are difficult to reach without the proper equipment, or without gaining entry to particular apartments.

b. Floodlight beams should be aimed at areas known to be nighttime drug haunts and should function with automatic clock switches.

c. In parking lots, alleys, schoolyards, and other areas frequented by druggies, place floodlights on any available perch, making sure that the area frequented is bathed in brightness.

4. The *intimidating physical presence* of a **uniformed Anti-druggie Patrol** should be a show of force symbolic of your neighborhood's total commitment to a druggie-free environment.

a. *The uniform* should be clearly visible, distinctive, and immediately identifiable. It does not have to be anything as elaborate as a police-type uniform, although some neighborhood conditions might warrant that. It should be a clear message to the drug buyer that *he* is the target of the organization. An example might be T-shirts with DRUG-BUYER IDENTIFICATION COMMITTEE across the front and back.

b. *The members should patrol in force.* Groups of four and five should be the minimum. (In some neighborhoods that minimum might be substantially higher.) Just the sight of this kind of group will be enough to send most frightened druggies scurrying across town. *And can you think of a better image for the community's kids to see and emulate?*

   c. *The patrol should be visibly well equipped.* Members should carry, at a minimum, walkie-talkies, cameras (conventional and/or video), bullhorns, and possibly handcuffs, and nightsticks provided you have already obtained proper training and instruction from your local police department regarding their use. Remember, this is a *show* of force.

   5. *Decoy cars* should be parked near druggie-frequented corners and/or buildings, with difficult-to-remove, glued paper signs plastering the windows. The signs might read:

DRUG BUYERS BEWARE!
THIS IS A BAD NEIGHBORHOOD TO PARK YOUR CARS WHEN YOU BUY DRUGS!
THIS CAR WAS USED TO VIOLATE FEDERAL AND STATE LAW.

   I guarantee that a couple of strategically placed cars, with these signs on them, will convince many car-borne druggies to look elsewhere for their drugs, and an equal number of dealers to look for more hassle-free terrain. It might also clear up your neighborhood's parking problems. From time to time it may become necessary to actually paste one of these signs on a druggie's car provided you have obtained proper instruction from your local authorities as to the use of such a tactic (this tactic is discussed next, in "Tactical Street Action").

   6. *Surveillance video cameras* should be set up in visible but difficult-to-reach locations such as the sides of buildings

or on utility poles. The presence of cameras—for visible threat purposes—is more important than how effectively they operate. You might even put up a bunch of cheap decoy cameras.

But you have to keep the druggies honest. A good way of doing that is periodically to film one of them making a buy from a hidden, well-protected OP—perhaps a darkened apartment window or the rear of a closed store. A day or two later the *sight* of poster-sized photos of people caught in the act of making a drug transaction, posted all over the neighborhood with a caption such as . . .

CAUGHT IN THE ACT!
THIS PHOTO OF A DRUG TRANSACTION TAKEN
ON (date)
HAS BEEN TURNED OVER TO THE POLICE.

. . . will have an amazingly sobering and location-changing effect on drug buyers. The paranoid druggies will be seeing cameras in every window whether they are there or not, and that is what we want!

As you can see, the methods and tactics for making your living space visibly inhospitable and frightening to drug buyers is only limited by your imagination. When a druggie enters your community it should be immediately evident that he's in a BAD place to be looking for a connection. In most cases a strong visible threat by itself will be enough to convince him to go elsewhere.

ANOTHER EXAMPLE OF THE EFFECTIVENESS OF VISIBLE THREAT

Dick Gregory, comedian and political activist, now active in the war on druggies, was aiding Shreveport, Louisiana, residents to rid themselves of drug buyers roving their neighborhoods in cars. Gregory operated out of a camper emblazoned with the words DRUG BUSTER, A DRUG-FREE ZONE. His plan was to scare drug buyers by taking down their license-plate numbers and giving them to the police. Wherever Gregory parked his camper, just the visible threat of his presence cut the drug trafficking in half.[1] If just the presence of this man and his camper cut trafficking in half, imagine how effective he would have been had he been able to turn the whole community into a Visible Threat zone.

TACTICAL STREET ACTION

To convince those few druggies who don't get the message that your neighborhood *really* is a BAD place to buy drugs, certain types of tactical street actions should be carried out with regularity. It is important to note that the recommendations listed below are general in nature. Each community—neighborhood, block, housing development, or building—has its own particular conditions, peculiarities, and personalities, and must be approached differently. What may be done safely and effectively in one neighborhood might be dangerous and ineffective in another. Keep in mind that the druggie and *not* the dealer is the enemy. Stick to that and you'll never go wrong.

For example, in neighborhoods with heavy street dealing, foot patrols might invite confrontation with dealers. To avoid this the group might employ a heavier use of visible signs; the imaginative use of loudspeakers from hidden OPs; and the isolation of the dealing area by citizens' patrols forming a cordon through which the druggies must pass to reach their dealers ("Circle of Fear" concept, to be dis-

[1] Penny Brown, "Thinning Out Drug Ranks," *USA Today,* 7/27/89.

cussed at length in section on suburban and rural action). Once again, the only limitations on the actions your group takes are the imagination and the law.

1. *Important preliminary measures*

It is important that *before* beginning foot and motorized patrols and other tactical street actions described below, your group take the following preliminary measures:

a. Request the permanent assignment of a member of local law enforcement as liaison with your organization. He or she will be an invaluable source of training, aid, and information.

b. Review group operational plans with the local police and district attorney's office for coordination and suggestions.

c. Review group operational plans with neighboring or other citizens' groups for coordination and mutual support.

d. Insure that every member of the group is furnished with twenty-four-hour emergency contact numbers for police, medical aid, other group members, and other citizens' groups.

e. Insure that each member is properly indoctrinated and has received all available training (as recommended in this book); and that each understands the primary goal of the group.

2. *General rules of tactical action*

It is imperative that the following general rules of tactical action be strictly adhered to:

a. *All* tactical action must be for the purpose of frightening, intimidating, and otherwise discouraging the *drug user* from entering your community to purchase drugs. The drug dealer is *not* your target—leave him to the police.

b. *All* tactical action must have as its primary goal *prevention, not provocation.* A citizens' antidrug patrol is—as much as humanly possible—the *show* of force, not the *use* of force.

3. *Equipment, manpower, and safety requirements for patrols*

a. A foot patrol should number from four to eight people (or more, depending on the amount of drug trafficking in the neighborhood), always staying together in a group.

b. A car patrol should never have fewer than three group members, and the car should be clearly marked with the organization's name and/or logo.

c. No group member should be permitted to patrol without wearing the group's uniform. The uniform is not only a deterrent to the druggie, it also enables police to immediately recognize group members.

d. The group should either be in direct radio contact with local police, via a hand-held portable radio (walkie-talkie), or to a group member's home equipped with a CB base radio station. (Just the sight of a walkie-talkie will avoid many incidents of possible physical confrontation.)

e. A citizens' patrol group should be armed with a camera—preferably a video camera—at all times. In twenty-five years of street enforcement I have found the pointing of a camera to be as effective in deterring mob violence as it is in frightening druggies. Ideally, a patrol group should carry both a conventional and a video camera.

f. All vehicles used for community patrol should be clearly marked with your organization's name and in themselves should represent a visible threat to the druggie. The vehicle should be equipped with CB radio equipment, flashlight, emergency light, loudspeaker system, and both a video and photo camera.

g. Building patrols, or security checkpoints, must have a minimum of three or more uniformed members with radio communications or immediate access to a telephone, loud whistles or air horns, and a camera. There are never too many members of a citizens' patrol. The more imposing the presence, the more effective the druggie deterrent.

STREET TACTICS

The community organization must never lose sight of the fact that they are most effective, first, as a visual threat. The more obvious the threat to the buyer, the more effective the deterrent. However, a visible threat with no teeth is no threat at all. Thus the group will periodically—more often at the beginning of the campaign—have to back up its *show* of force and fury with *real* street action. Of course, this does not mean you will be pursuing physical confrontation with a druggie target. As a general rule, if a situation seems as if it *may* become confrontational, you want to retreat and call the police immediately. The following list of recommended street tactics may be varied, improved upon, and adopted for use in any street-level drug-trafficking situation. Once again, the only limitations are your imagination and the law.

1. *Use of bullhorns and loudspeakers*
Noise used as a tactical weapon to terrify and confuse an enemy has long been used in warfare. Veterans of the Korean War will never forget the Chinese army's blowing what sounded like thousands of bugles through loudspeakers as a prelude to their massive human-horde suicide attacks. The sometimes hours-long periods of shrieking horns jangled even the most steely-nerved veterans. "Man, when those

horns blew, you just wanted to be anywhere else on the face of the earth," a veteran of that war once told me. His words described precisely the feeling a BAD organization wants to instill in any druggie entering its community's boundaries.

It was purely by accident that I stumbled on the potential power of noise as weapon in the war on drugs. In the summer of 1987 I was in charge of a raiding party of some twenty DEA agents in eight or nine vehicles. We were to make a series of crack and cocaine dealer arrests in Washington Heights—a section of New York City that is one of the most dangerous, drug-infested neighborhoods in the United States. Most of the area's dealers specialize in crack and cocaine, and are armed illegal aliens who have very little fear of the law. In just one night in October 1988 two New York City cops were killed by drug dealers in separate incidents only blocks apart.

As my squad circled the area in undercover cars (sports cars, vans, taxicabs, luxury cars), several of the people for whom we had arrest warrants were spotted on West 160th Street, between Broadway and Amsterdam Avenue. It was my job to give the "hit" signal. I turned onto the block, alone, driving a sporty two-tone Camaro equipped with a government radio hidden in the glove compartment, and a siren and loudspeaker beneath the hood. With a flick of a hand switch I could use the microphone—at that moment gripped tightly in my sweaty hand, held low in my lap so that it couldn't be seen from outside—to either transmit messages over the radio, or bellow orders out onto the street through the loudspeaker. I didn't know it then, but I had the switch flipped in the wrong direction.

As I rolled slowly up the street, literally swarming with druggies and dealers, I spotted two of our "subjects," busily engaged in selling drugs. There was no telling how long they would stay put, so I decided to call the hit. I squeezed the mike button in my lap. "IS EVERYONE IN POSITION?" I yelled, bobbing my head up and down and grinning like a clown. If any of the lookouts, steerers, and dealers were watching me, they'd think I was singing to the radio.

I thought.

I heard the sound of my own voice echoing back at me off the canyon-like walls. *But how could that be?*

I let the car roll slowly forward. It seemed like everyone on the block was staring at me. None of my men had responded. The two subjects were staring bug eyed, right at me. No sense faking it anymore. I squeezed the mike button angrily. "IS EVERYONE IN GODDAMNED POSITION? RESPOND!" My voice exploded around me like a depth bomb. People were suddenly moving off cars and stoops and heading into alleys and buildings. I stared at the mike in my lap. My heart sank. The switch was on loudspeaker. I looked out at the street. Not only had the subjects disappeared, but so had ninety percent of the people on the street.

I had to postpone the arrests for that day. I had burned the "set" badly. Street informants later told us that there would probably be little drug dealing on the block for the rest of the day, or maybe even a day or two. Later the thought occurred to me that if I could clear *that* meanest of mean streets of bad-ass drug dealers with nothing more than a loudspeaker, I was sure that its use in the hands of a civilian patrol could quickly clear *any* street of the paranoid, easily frightened druggies.

a. *The use of bullhorns on foot patrol*

The creative use of a bullhorn, carried by a roving community antidruggie patrol, in itself can sharply reduce drug trafficking in any area. Once again, its use is only limited by your imagination. The important thing to remember is NEVER to use it to confront dealers.

EXAMPLE OF A GROUP'S USE OF BULLHORNS ON FOOT PATROL

I was recently made aware of a citizens' organization in one of the most drug-infested areas of the South Bronx, the "Morris Avenue Block Patrol Antidrug Crew," which has already instituted the use of bullhorn patrols with great success. The biggest and most intimidating members patrol their block in groups of four and five, wearing their neighborhood association's T-shirts and carrying large battery-powered bullhorns. This group of courageous New Yorkers, however, are in the risky business of confronting the drug dealers—something I do not recommend. When they spot a known dealer the members walk toward him en masse, announcing with electronically amplified voices: "DEALER ON THE BLOCK!" The dealers usually leave.[1]

The operation, so far, is successful, but *not* because the dealers are frightened off. This group, aside from presenting a very formidable *visible threat,* has already received a lot of notoriety through the media. Druggies have stopped going into their area to shop because they don't want to go through this kind of hassle, especially when there are so many trouble-free locations to buy drugs from. Nowadays the belief that you can confront and frighten dealers off your block is one that has already cost too many lives.

I recommend that, instead of approaching drug dealers—most of whom by their actions will already be known, or suspected, by your group—turn your attention to the transients whom you suspect as potential drug buyers, point the bullhorn in their direction and say, "DRUG BUYERS ON THE BLOCK! DRUG BUYERS ON THE BLOCK! THE

[1] "Making a Difference, Block by City Block," *The New York Times,* 4/30/89.

POLICE ARE BEING NOTIFIED!" But never forget: Avoid confrontation. If a situation looks like it *may* turn confrontational, retreat and call the police.

To keep the buyers honest—if they don't keep moving—call the police. There are laws against vagrancy, loitering, and loitering with intent to buy drugs, in every state. With a member of your group as complainant, the local police will have the right to question and possibly search anyone you identify as "acting in a suspicious or furtive manner." In all likelihood you won't have to do this too many times before the word gets around that your community is a BAD place to buy drugs. But in any event, do not hesitate to call the police as many times as you feel necessary. It is *your* community you are defending; and *you* are paying the police to be a vital part of that defense.

b. *Loudspeakers activated from observation posts*

This is a technique that can be particularly useful in heavy-drug-trafficking communities. It can virtually eliminate the possibility of confrontation with the dealers and at the same time create an environment few druggies would dare to enter.

TYPE, INSTALLATION, AND POSITIONING OF LOUDSPEAKERS

Loudspeakers of the outdoor, all-weather variety (as powerful as can be obtained), should be rigged to broadcast radio-transmitted voices originating from concealed or distant locations. The loudspeakers should be permanently affixed high up on the sheer face of apartment buildings, on well-secured rooftops; or installed on utility poles or even tall trees. They should be protected by a wire protective assembly (or something similar). A minimum of two or three should be installed on any given block. The business end of the speakers should be facing (projecting toward) known drug-dealing locations.

Radio transmitters, capable of voice broadcasting over the loudspeakers, should be portable and have a range of at least a quarter mile. Thus they may be moved from one observation post to another or even activated from a car or the rear of a van. All the equipment is readily available through electronic-equipment dealers.

OBSERVATION POST SECURITY

The precautions taken in concealing observation posts and the identities of those making direct observations on drug-dealing locations depend on how dangerous and aggressive the drug dealers of your community really are. Once you've begun your deterrent action and buyers have begun to look elsewhere for their drugs, you will find that many dealers will quickly abandon the community. My experience has shown me that if you haven't confronted them directly, retribution won't even occur to them—it's bad business. Your need for security will quickly disappear. You will be recapturing your own living space. However, at the beginning of your antidruggie campaign I would suggest the following security precautions be taken:

a. In general, apartments, or other locations used as observation posts—from which the loudspeakers may be activated—should have windows with curtains, drapes, plants and foliage, and/or other camouflage to hide those surveilling the street.

b. At least two people should man the observation post. One should be free to speak over the loudspeaker, maintain radio contact with other members of the group posted on the street, or to call the police if necessary. The other remains at the window making observations and reporting what he sees.

c. Observation posts may be as distant as a quarter mile away from the drug-dealing location, if adequate spyglass equipment is on hand.

The idea is to create a nameless, faceless, BOOMING threat to the druggies and avoid confrontation with the dealers.

A HYPOTHETICAL EXAMPLE

A druggie in a bright blue sweatsuit has braved all your neighborhood warning signs and shuffles toward a basement your BAD organization has identified as a drug-dealing location. He pauses at the entrance and nervously checks the street. There are a half-dozen dealers and lookouts on the street checking for police.

"YOU IN THE BLUE SWEATSUIT," booms a voice from a loudspeaker attached to the sheer wall of a building across the street. It is one of a half-dozen speakers strategically posted on the block. "POSSESSION OF NARCOTICS IS A FELONY! WE ARE CALLING THE POLICE WITH YOUR DESCRIPTION RIGHT NOW! WHEN YOU COME OUT OF THAT BASEMENT THE POLICE WILL ALREADY BE HERE!"

The druggie looks around. There is no way he can tell where the voice is coming from. He doesn't hesitate a beat. His cocaine-frazzled brain goes into paranoid overdrive. His heartbeat explodes to about two hundred per. He sees undercover narcs under every car and watching him from every window. He high-steps his sorry butt out of your living space as fast as his legs will carry him. It won't be long before all his friends know what a hassle it is to buy drugs in YOUR community. And it won't be long before the dealer is also looking for another, more lucrative location.

2. *Use of cameras and video cameras*

I discovered the powerful antidruggie weapon a camera can be in a very curious way. During a midsummer 1975 heroin raid in a teeming, drug-infested south Brooklyn ghetto, a large, ugly mob formed outside a garage where we had just made five arrests.

I was one of about ten or eleven agents holding five prisoners and about a half pound of heroin inside the sweltering sheet-metal garage. Outside there were a couple of hundred heat-crazed people—a good portion of them junkies—waiting for us to try and make it across the street to our double-parked cars. The guy running the raid decided that the best thing for us to do was just grab our prisoners and rush headlong for our cars, as quickly as we could. His theory was that the crowd—not having a leader—would not have time to react.

Nice theory.

As we started onto the street, the crowd shifted like a giant football line and blocked the way to our cars. I turned and found the way back to the garage also blocked. I heard the ragged-out voice of some druggie shout, "Get the pigs! Get the pigs!" Others joined in.

To this day I'm not sure why I did it. I mean, it wasn't a conscious thought or anything; I just reached into my shoulder bag and brought out a little camera that I always carried with me to photograph raid scenes and evidence. I aimed it at the people immediately in front of me and started to click away. They ducked their heads and pushed out of the way as if they were Nazi war criminals or Mafia capos. What they really were was a bunch of paranoid junkies. I aimed the camera to the right and left of me and it was as if the reaction was catching. I was aiming my camera and half the street was running and ducking. Our little platoon started laughing; even some of the handcuffed prisoners were laughing. In a flash we were in our cars and moving. I was still aiming and clicking my camera and people were still ducking.

I thought I had discovered the "atomic bomb" of crowd-control weapons. It was not until years later that I realized what I had really discovered: The common camera is one hell of a druggie repellent. The paranoia of druggies can never be overstated. A camera pointed in the direction of a druggie is an object of such terror that some—and I've seen this—will duck and hurl their bodies suicidally through fast-moving traffic. In a lot of cases the fear may be caused by the druggie's having committed more crimes than he can remember to support his habit. But—it bears repeating—the vast majority of our nation's druggies are so-called "straights" with jobs and families who simply do not want to be discovered and exposed. But again, the rule is that if a situation appears that it *may* turn confrontational, back out and call the police.

Thus, the antidruggie patrol should be armed with at least one conventional and/or video camera, and plenty of film. Do not be shy about photographing *anyone* suspected of being in your community to buy drugs, or about telling him, or her, *why* you are photographing them. Signs posted around the community should have already forewarned them that SUSPECTED DRUG BUYERS WILL BE PHOTO-GRAPHED AND THEIR PHOTOS TURNED OVER TO THE PO-LICE.

If you make a mistake and photograph a "solid citizen," no harm done. *"We're sorry, Mac; where should we send the photos?"* If the guy's not *really* as innocent as he claims, you can bet you've captured one druggie on film whom you will never see again.

Video cameras are now smaller, more durable, and easier to operate than ever before. If a video camera is available to the group, use it. The terror druggies have for cameras is magnified when it's a video camera.

3. *Combined use of camera and bullhorn*

The use of both bullhorn and camera at the same time may be more than the heart of the average druggie can stand.

A HYPOTHETICAL EXAMPLE

Your patrol has observed a man enter a house known to be a drug-dealing location. After about ten minutes the man leaves. Your group is waiting for him about a block away. As he approaches, you suddenly surround him. Two members begin taking his picture (or videotaping him) from various angles, while another yells through a bullhorn, "THIS MAN IS SUSPECTED OF JUST HAVING BOUGHT DRUGS! WE HAVE TAKEN HIS PHOTO! SOMEONE CALL A POLICE OFFICER! et cetera, et cetera."

You then do your public best to get the man arrested by a police officer. If you fail, don't worry about it; it will snow in Miami before he, or anyone he knows, returns to your community to buy drugs. Druggies talk to each other; they have a grapevine as efficient as AP, UPI, and The New York Times.

4. *Community patrol vehicles*

The use of manned, well-marked antidruggie patrol vehicles is a powerful deterrent to buyers. Most druggies—every druggie I have ever known—on seeing that they are under the scrutiny of men in radio cars will keep on moving. The use of vehicles is an added deterrent to those drug buyers cruising the community in cars. The creative use of car, camera, and bullhorn can quickly and drastically reduce the number of mobile drug customers in any area.

For instance, can you imagine the effect on the line of drug customers sitting in their cars in front of the 109th Street location, if a citizens' patrol car rolled slowly by, photographing or filming each driver, and announcing over the bullhorn that each license-plate number and photo was being turned over to the police? These were the same people who wailed, *"What will I do if my family finds out?"* when they were arrested. The possible uses of car, camera, and bullhorn in a creative druggie-deterrent program are limitless.

A HYPOTHETICAL EXAMPLE

Duane Sleaze, a bank teller, has just bought a couple of vials of crack from an apartment in a building in your neighborhood. He leaves the building, nervously checking the street, and quickly crosses to his car. One of your street informants signals you in your OP. You grab the mike of a CB radio or portable phone and contact a car waiting two blocks behind him with four "bad"-looking members of a neighboring BAD organization.

Duane, already drooling in expectation of his next high, pulls the car away from the curb, mindless of a nondescript car following him. As he drives, he happily rolls the little vials of "love drug" around in his fingertips.

A car, with a woman driving, cuts in front of Duane and slows. There's some kind of writing all over the car but he just can't get the big letters to focus in his mind. He tries to pass, but is blocked by another car with big letters on it and four men in it. The traffic light turns red; the woman stops and

Duane is wedged in. Something is wrong. There is sudden movement from the car alongside. The window rolls down and Duane finds himself facing a huge man with a bullhorn!

"YOU IN THE RED TOYOTA," booms the voice.

"Me?" Duane mouths the word, the vials of crack now gripped tightly in his sweating hand.

"YOU JUST BOUGHT CRACK IN 1975 HONEYWELL AVENUE. WE HAVE NOTIFIED THE POLICE WITH YOUR DESCRIPTION AND YOUR LICENSE-PLATE NUMBER!"

A cop on the beat steps off the curb and peers curiously at the scene.

"OFFICER! OFFICER! THE MAN IN THE RED TOYOTA HAS JUST BOUGHT DRUGS!" booms the voice. Before the cop has taken one curious step forward, a very sick-looking Duane has somehow managed to swallow ten plastic vials filled with crack, in one terrified gulp. You can bet that—if he survives—neither he nor anyone he knows will ever return to your neighborhood.

In that one action you will have done more damage to drug trafficking in YOUR neighborhood than the extradition of any hundred Colombian drug barons.

4. *Use of Stickem signs*

We have all seen the almost-impossible-to-remove Stickem signs posted on illegally parked cars. Their creative use against drug buyers' vehicles can work wonders in clearing up your druggie-congested streets. Although some citizens are already using this tactic, you should obtain prior instruction and training from your local authorities before instituting this or any of the tactics in this book to make sure you're applying them properly. I suggest something in a bright red or yellow, with bold black lettering that reads:

THIS VEHICLE WAS USED TO PURCHASE ILLEGAL DRUGS IN (Your community). THIS IS A BAD PLACE TO BUY DRUGS. THE LICENSE NUMBER HAS BEEN TURNED OVER TO LAW-ENFORCEMENT AUTHORITIES.

5. *Citizen's arrest and physical confrontation*

All American citizens have the right—no, the duty—to make a citizen's arrest when they observe a serious crime being committed in their presence and there are no police available. There are some citizen patrol organizations like the Guardian Angels who actively exercise that right. But in order that your group members are prepared for any eventuality, advice and training should be obtained from local prosecutors, law enforcement authorities, and experienced citizen action groups before engaging in citizens' arrests. For the purposes of a BAD organization I recommend that citizen's arrest powers *not* be used as a matter of policy, but only as a last resort in the following circumstances:

a. If a member of the group is assaulted and police are unavailable for the arrest. *My long experience as both a narcotics agent and as a martial-arts expert has taught me that the more intimidating and businesslike your group appears, the less likelihood there will be of any physical confrontations, particularly in situations involving frightened and paranoid druggies.*

b. Police absolutely refuse to arrest drug buyers, as a matter of policy, in spite of clear evidence that they (the druggies) have violated the law.

In all likelihood—if your organization mounts an effective Visible Threat campaign, combined with street tactics and good police liaison—your community will be devoid of druggies and dealers long before either physical confrontations occur or citizen's arrest action is ever necessary. The following are some hypothetical examples, followed by some suggested guidelines for the actual use of citizen's arrest powers:

EXAMPLE OF A SITUATION LEADING TO A PHYSICAL CONFRONTATION AND CITIZEN'S ARREST

Let's say a known druggie has braved your Visible Threat zone and makes a buy from a street dealer. A group member has filmed the drugs and money changing hands from an apartment across the street. Six members of your group follow the druggie out of the area, away from any possible confrontation with the dealer, and suddenly surround him. "We just observed you buying drugs in front of 1975 Honeywell Avenue," says the patrol leader. "You either turn them over to us or we are calling the police!" The guy, without a word, suddenly charges through your group, knocking one of the members to the pavement:

"THAT MAN JUST BOUGHT DRUGS! SOMEONE CALL THE POLICE," bellows one of your members over the bullhorn, running behind him while another contacts a group member seated near a phone ready for emergencies, via CB radio, who, in turn, calls the police. Now the guy is running full tilt, but your group is staying right behind him. He takes a couple of tubes of crack out of his pocket and throws them away. Two members of the group—the weakest and slowest—drop back to grab the evidence while the others continue in pursuit, still blasting away on the bullhorn, "SOMEONE CALL A COP. THIS MAN JUST ASSAULTED SOMEONE! HE HAS DRUGS ON HIM!"

The guy suddenly stops, turns, and approaches one of your group. At this point you may have to make a citizen's arrest and physically detain him until police arrive. If you followed the instructions in this book you will have two or three people on the scene who are trained and capable of handling such a situation. This type of situation should be extremely rare. The idea is to create a hostile environment not a hostile situation. Obviously, if the druggie appears at all dangerous, you should retreat and call the police.

It's important to note, right here, that the situation described did not have to be pushed to that extreme. Once the druggie ran, the group could have let him go and still achieved its goal. He would be one druggie who would never return to that community. *Who needs that kind of hassle?*

In most cases citizen's arrest powers will not have to be used. But it makes good sense to be well prepared for all eventualities. In some hard-core druggie areas—areas frequented by garbage heads, and crack and heroin addicts—the need for citizens' arrests may be more likely. However, even in these areas, once the word gets around that it's a hassle to buy drugs, the druggies will soon shift to other locales, and the sellers will follow.

My general guidelines for the use of citizen's arrest powers are as follows:

a. Citizen's arrest powers should only be exercised in those instances where you have overwhelming evidence of the crime, such as a videotape of the actual drug transaction.

b. *Never, under any circumstances,* should an attempt be made to arrest drug dealers.

c. Drug buyers should be confronted *after* they have left the vicinity of the purchase, insuring that the action is nonconfrontational with the drug dealer. And avoid confronting any drug buyer who appears dangerous. If a situation seems as if it may become confrontational, retreat and call the police.

d. As a planned tactic a citizen's arrest should *only* be attempted when there are members of the group present who have been trained in the martial arts and/or police work, and, of course, only after the group has obtained prior training and instruction as to the use of citizen's arrest powers from local law enforcement and prosecutors' offices.

EXAMPLE OF UNORTHODOX BUT SUCCESSFUL STREET TACTIC

The following is a true-life example of how a community organization acting within the parameters of the law is only limited in its tactics by its own collective imagination and desire to do the job; and how the most confrontational of situations can be handled nonviolently.

"STARE" TACTICS

A group of angry citizens, residents of town houses and luxurious high-rise apartment buildings on New York's East Side, awoke one day to find that their neighborhood was fast becoming a marketplace for drugs. Unafraid of police action and certain that upper-income people would, at worst, call the police, drug dealers turned the affluent blocks bounded by 29th and 30th streets, Park Avenue South and Lexington Avenue, into a wide-open drug-dealing bazaar.

The local residents reacted at first—just as the drug dealers had thought they would—by flooding the police, suits, and politicians with phone calls, complaints, and letters that, in turn, resulted in more examples of how impotent and fictitious our war on drugs really is. A bunch of useless arrests were made and before the dealers could jump bail, there were others fighting each other for the street corners. It was the 92nd Street Block Association's experience repeated, as it is repeated thousands of times a day throughout our nation.

But this particular group was not going to stop there. They would not be dissuaded by the suits throwing their hands up in surrender and claiming that more funds for education and rehabilitation were needed, and all the other baloney most of us have heard so often that we know it by heart. They decided to take the destiny of their living environment into their own hands. Their neighborhood was becoming a nightmare and they wanted immediate action. One of the residents described the situation perfectly in an article that appeared in *The New York Times:*

> "I've lived here since 1981, and suddenly, when night came, the streets no longer belonged to us," said Kathy Goforth, as she patrolled with twenty neighbors. With the influx of drug sellers, Ms. Goforth, a public relations consultant, said the area began to resemble a rain-forest society.
>
> "We the tenants were like the occupants of trees, living above in apartments," she said. "And the streets had become the territory of the dealers and crack heads."[1]

Sound familiar, America?
The group decided to confront *the dealers* (in the words

[1] Selwyn Raab, "East Side Drug Patrol's Tactic: Stare," *The New York Times,* 9/5/89.

of one of the members), "in a nonviolent manner"—a tactic that might have resulted in tragedy, but luckily did not.

The group, numbering from twenty to thirty, took to the streets, in nightly patrols, carrying posters that read, NO CRACK, NO DRUGS WANTED HERE, et cetera, et cetera. The members would single out the easily recognizable drug dealers and stand near them in what another member described as a "nonintimidating posture," saying nothing and simply staring at them from a distance of about twenty feet. The results were quick and gratifying—the dealers left. But not before giving the upstart organization a street name: "the Blockos."

The newspaper article reported that the group had defeated "the drug dealers." They had indeed, but the important point missed by both the reporter and the organization was that the dealers had not abandoned the neighborhood out of fear, intimidation, or the threat of imminent arrest and exposure. They left because the drug buyers, on entering the block and seeing the sign-carrying citizens—a VISIBLE THREAT of being hassled and exposed—decided to take their business elsewhere. With no customers the sellers had no reason to stay.

The Blockos, in their refusal to leave their futures and the condition of their home turf in the hands of politicians and suits, and their willingness to turn the energy of their anger and frustration into meaningful action, exhibited what the block-by-block winning of this druggie war is all about and that, in the majority of cases, a visible threat may be enough to win the war in your neighborhood.

STRATEGIC TACTICS

For a community to be successful in ridding its streets of drug abuse over the long haul it will have to become involved in other activities, tactics, and strategies that may take them far from the streets of their communities. Activities that garner the support of the justice system, the media, the politicians, and most important: that of other like-minded community organizations.

Getting Justice from the Justice System

For twenty-five years as a narcotics agent I have watched our justice system become a bigger enemy in this war on drugs than any drug dealer I have ever met. I have seen the biggest drug dealers alive make plea-bargain agreements and receive jail sentences that screamed, CRIME PAYS. I've heard judges advocate the legalization of drugs and refuse to sentence drug dealers. I once went through two complete federal trials (the first ended in a mistrial), testifying against a dangerous drug dealer with a long arrest record, who had sold me a half pound of heroin, only to have the judge—after the guy was found guilty—sentence him to "time served," which meant his immediate release.[1] I have watched judges deport South American drug smugglers who had already been caught two and three times in the past under different names and deported. I have witnessed the CIA and other intelligence agencies—for their own clandestine reasons—secretly obtain the release from jail of some of the biggest drug dealers alive.[2] And in all my years in this war on drugs I have yet to see one single drug buyer prosecuted.

In short, our drug laws, as a deterrent to the user, are

[1] Donald Goddard, *Undercover* (New York: Times Books, 1988). (Judge Constance Baker Motley.)
[2] Michael Levine, *Deep Cover* (New York: Delacorte Press, 1989).

nonexistent. The BAD organization must do everything in its power in its own community to change this.

Getting the cooperation of the justice system is probably going to be one of the most difficult tasks an organization will encounter. I can guarantee one thing, though: It will give you the opportunity to witness, firsthand, one of the chief reasons our war on drugs is laughed at around the world. Do not allow setbacks to dishearten you. They should inspire your members to work harder to show our bureaucrats and elected officials—those responsible for the naming of our judges—the kind of anti–drug-abuse effort we really want.

To further demonstrate that your community is a BAD one for drug shopping, your organization should follow every arrest through the entire legal system—from arraignment to sentencing—exercising every bit of influence it can at every level of the process, to insure that every druggie arrested in your neighborhood is dealt with as severely as possible. The formation of a committee with this as their primary responsibility is extremely important.

This tactic is nothing new. Citizens' groups all over the country are beginning to recognize that without the backing of the criminal justice system, community action—even against the druggies—will eventually fail. It's like aiming a gun that everyone knows is empty. Thus many organizations, as an important part of their activities, are making their presence "felt" in the justice system. But here again, many are making the same mistake our leaders are making, and focusing their attention on drug dealers. The druggies are all but forgotten. I found a great example of this right here in New York.

The Neighborhood Anti-Crime Center, of New York, an umbrella organization for New York City's ten thousand community, block, and building associations, has a special program devoted to aiding these organizations to "fight drugs." As part of the program they distribute pamphlets with tips and suggestions on how each group can be more effective at all levels of their "antidrug" efforts. One of these pamphlets, called "Getting Justice from the Criminal Justice System," counsels community organizations that the knowledge in the pamphlet will lead to *"quality arrests that don't end up with a revolving door for the drug dealer."*

This huge citizens' organization has swallowed the Big Lie, hook, line, and sinker. The arrest and prosecution of the druggie is overlooked entirely. Sadly, it reflects the thinking of the majority of citizens' organizations around the country and causes these groups to waste resources and man-hours in futile efforts at getting dealers—who have long since been replaced on their streets by other dealers— long prison sentences. If this same effort were expended on all *drug-user* arrests, more damage would be done to the drug business than if the entire Medellín cartel were assassinated in one night.

1. *Designation of a justice committee*

To get the most out of the criminal justice system the community organization should designate a special committee whose *only* function should be doing all it can to make the justice system a deterrent for drug users. The members of this committee should be prepared to follow the progress of each druggie arrest through the three levels of the system —law enforcement, prosecution, and judicial—and insure that the group's influence is felt at each of these levels.

2. *Law enforcement*

Your group's actions will cause the arrests of druggies, who in all likelihood will only have small, user amounts of drugs, or no drugs at all and only drug paraphernalia (crack pipes, coke spoon, syringe, and so on). The arrests will have occurred—in most cases—as a result of the police being called to the scene on the basis of your group's observations and telephone and/or radio calls; or in some cases as a result of your group's exercising its citizen's arrest authority. Some police officers may not want to be bothered with a "minor" drug arrest, and may try to convince you to drop charges.

Never agree to this.

In *all* cases full prosecution should be insisted upon.

In most states there are vagrancy, loitering, and loitering-with-intent-to-buy-drugs statutes. If by chance no drugs are found on a druggie whose search and/or detention your group has caused, *insist* that one of these other charges be used and assure the police that your group will press all charges and act as witnesses. Make sure the druggie is witness to your dogged insistence in his prosecution.

Be prepared for plenty of disappointment. If you insist—as you must—the cop on the street will have to make the arrest, but in all likelihood, district attorneys will refuse to prosecute and the druggie will be released. But take heart, he has spent at least a couple of hours in jail, and when released he will spread the "BAD" word about your organization to other druggies. Take it from a guy who's spent his life in this business: Your action will have inflicted serious damage to the local drug dealer's business.

Exert Political Pressure for Law-Enforcement Operations Targeting Buyers

My long career in narcotics enforcement has shown me time and again that drug enforcement is *the* most politically affected branch of law enforcement in our nation's history. All the enforcement programs, from international to local levels, are reflections of political promises and agendas. Just as the 92nd Street Block Association was able, through Congressman Rangel, to get the Drug Enforcement Administration to mount a full-scale—albeit failed—operation against the local street dealers, *you* can get your local police to mount an enforcement operation against drug buyers.

Reverse Undercover Operation

A type of law enforcement operation all community organizations should be aware of is the "reverse undercover operation," which entails undercover officers posing as dealers and selling drugs to unwary buyers and then arresting them for "possession," a felony in most states. "Reverses," as narcotics enforcement professionals refer to them, are always successful in cleaning up drug trafficking in *any* community where they are implemented; as are most buyer-oriented operations. Yet the few law-enforcement administrators who institute them *always* run into stiff opposition from prosecutors and politicians, still mired in the "big bust," "media mileage," "that-doesn't-win-votes" mentality —the Big Lie.[1] (Reverse undercover and other druggie-oriented enforcement approaches are discussed in more detail in chapter 4, devoted to suburban antidruggie tactics.)

To begin changing attitudes your group must be unremitting in contacting local politicians and showing them that— as a group—you will vote against them and influence all you know to do likewise, unless they exercise whatever influence they can in getting the police to mount full-scale enforcement efforts against the drug buyers in your community.

---

[1] One of the more notable exponents of "reverse undercover operations" is Sheriff Nick Navarro of Broward County, Florida.

Visible Police Presence

Political and media pressure exerted by drug-blighted urban neighborhood and community organizations will inevitably result in periodic police saturation operations, like the TNT (Tactical Narcotics Team) program and Operation Pressure Point in New York City, Operation Cul-de-Sac in Los Angeles, and many other similar operations run mostly by urban police forces across the nation. Squads of uniformed police are sent in to reclaim the streets of a neighborhood like a conquering army. And the streets—for however long the police maintain the operation—remain drug and crime free.

The people are led to believe that the operations are effective because the dealers are somehow frightened out of business. What actually happens is that dealers are forced out of business by the reluctance of druggies to enter areas so *visibly threatening* to them—"hot" areas. But as soon as the operation's funding runs out, or "significant" arrests drop, the troops are called back. Within days the area "cools" and the druggies and dealers return in force; and it's business as usual.

So, if all was for naught, what's the point in exerting pressure for police action?

The point is that in communities with BAD organizations, after the police leave, the organization's presence maintains the "heat" with its Visible Threat tactics, and the druggies do *not* return.

Recommendation

Thus in drug-blighted urban areas it is recommended that the BAD organization exert all its political influence to obtain *any* type of police saturation operation they can get.

Once the streets are reclaimed from the druggie, they are yours to hold. And as any military tactician knows—holding is a lot easier than conquering.

3. *Prosecution* (after *all* druggie arrests in your community).

The next step, after an arrest is made, is to transfer the case to a prosecutor (state: district, county, town, or village attorney; federal: an assistant United States attorney). Most local prosecutors—with the exception of the local United States attorney, who is appointed by the President—are elected officials and will respond to a community that can demonstrate solidarity and voting power. At first this may be difficult and at times disappointing. But the community's voting power *will* win out in the end.

Your request is a simple and straightforward one: You want *all* druggies arrested in *your* community prosecuted to the full limits of the law. To back up this request and make it easier for prosecutors to work with you, the committee your group has designated to devote its efforts to working closely with the justice system should:

a. Work closely with prosecutors

Request the prosecutor's advice and counsel in training the members of your group as witnesses; that is, the kind of observations, notes, written statements, and testimony they will need from you to successfully prosecute the case in court. There's not that much to it. Believe me. After your members have been through one or two prosecutions they will all be experts. And once you get the prosecutors on your side, the police will be more than happy to help you out.

b. Follow up on all arrests

Insure that the prosecutors know you mean business, and that this movement is not like most of the others that soon become more social and philanthropic than action oriented, by following up on the court dispositions of all drug arrests in your community. Keep records of every arrest and request that the local prosecutors account for the dispensation of each.

4. *Court appearances*

Now is when the fun really begins. The objective here is for the group, using whatever power it can muster, to pressure judges into treating druggies as harshly as the law will allow. This will be a great education for the group in what a lunacy and farce our war on drugs really is. You will be told everything from "There's no room in the jails" to "I think drugs should be legalized." Your position must be:

> "With all due respect, Your Honor, drugs *are illegal,* and we as a community deserve to be protected from the kind of conditions that follow wherever *drug users* shop for their wares. Thirty years of arresting dealers and fighting an overseas war on drugs has been a failure; we would like to try a different approach in *our* community."

You are going to win a few cases but lose most. But as to your overall objective of letting the druggies know what a hassle it is to enter your community, you will be a big winner.

In the end, what will convince our courts to stop treating the user as a victim is political clout. If your organization can muster enough voting strength, I can guarantee that most judges will feel a strong "urge" to do its bidding. And if the judge in your community is an elected official, you'll have no problem at all.

a. Recommended tactical actions in the court system
(1) *Attend all court hearings en masse.*
In general an arrested druggie will have four different types of court dates: the bail hearing, the arraignment, the trial, and, hopefully, the sentencing. These
are public hearings, and your organization should
muster as many uniformed members as it can to attend every one of these procedures. Again, the obvious showing of community anger, strength, unity,
and resolve will impress both the judge *and* the
druggie world. Win or lose, it is the kind of message
you want spread everywhere.
(2) *Testify whenever given the opportunity.*
The judges, justices, and magistrates at these hearings may or may not allow community representatives to speak to express the community's concerns
about the case. Usually the simple presence of a large
group will speak for itself; however, a spokesman for
the group should be designated to ask for permission
to speak. (The request *must* be coordinated with the
prosecuting attorney.) Thus it is important that the
group elect the most effective spokesperson among
you, who can deliver a short, succinct message, expressing the damage that drug-trafficking activity is
doing to your community and your group's belief
that *it is the druggie, first and foremost, who is responsible for it.*

b. Types of court procedures and tactics and goals at
each
(1) *Bail hearing*
A judge or magistrate reads the defendant the specifics of what he has been charged with and then deter-
mines—by weighing the gravity of the charges (pos-

sible sentence) against the defendant's roots in the community (job, family, bank accounts, et cetera)—the likelihood of his not appearing for trial. The higher the likelihood of flight, the higher the bail set.

The community organization should exert as much pressure as they can, with both the prosecutor and judge, to see that the highest bail possible is set. Always remember that whether you win or lose, there will usually be plenty of denizens of the drug world at these hearings, and the message your actions will be delivering—our neighborhood is a BAD place to buy drugs!—will be as important as the outcome.

(2) *Arraignment*

This is the court procedure during which the defendant is formally accused of the crime and is allowed to plead innocent or guilty. If he or she pleads *guilty* to the charges, the next hearing will be for sentencing. If the plea is *innocent,* the next court session will be for trial. If the defendant has already been able to raise bail money and is free, his attorney will request that he be "continued on bail" or ask for a "reduction of bail." If he has not been able to raise bail money his attorney will ask for a reduction of bail.

In either of the above instances the BAD organization (coordinating their actions with the prosecutor) must exert all the pressure it can for the judge to keep the druggie defendant in jail.

(3) *The trial*

A drug trial may be before a jury or only a judge. The choice is the defendant's to make. The Neighborhood Anti-Crime Center of New York counsels all its ten thousand affiliate groups: "You and your neighbors may attend the trial, and your presence will have an impact on the judge."[1] I could not agree with them more. You will have the same impact on a jury, which more than likely will be composed of a lot of people from your community or neighboring communities.

It is also important that your group display solidarity and support for its members or any other citizens of your community who might be testifying witnesses. Here again, you can bet that the courtroom will be filled with many of the defendant's druggie friends. Your community's message to *them* will be clear.

(4) *Sentencing*

Needless to say, this is a very important date. Your captured druggie has pled guilty, or been convicted after trial, and now faces the judge for his comeuppance. Once again (coordinating all efforts with the prosecutor), you must attempt to influence the judge in every legal way possible. Some courts allow the submission of written affidavits, and/or testimony, on behalf of the community, attesting to the harm caused by the defendant's drug-buying activity. Do both. This is yet another opportunity to send your community's message to the world: *Our community is a BAD place to buy drugs.*

"Remember: when a prosecutor takes a case to the court, he or she is said to represent 'the people' against the defendant. If your neighborhood group knows how

[1] Tim Wall, Neighborhood Anti-Crime Center pamphlet, entitled "Getting Justice from the Criminal Justice System." Published by Citizens for a Greater New York, 3 West 29 Street, New York, New York 10001.

**the criminal justice system works, you can make sure
that the voice of the people is heard."[1]**

The Community Group and the Media

All efforts should be made to acquire as many "friends"
in the media—newspapers, television, radio—as possible.
This should not be difficult. An urban community successfully combating drugs is news and the media will seek you
out. To use them to your advantage, four objectives should
be kept in mind.

First, you want your community to be notorious as a
terrible place for druggies to do their shopping. Second, you
want the politicians to take note of your voting power and
your ability to affect the vote of other like-minded communities. Third, you want the names and actions of judges,
prosecutors, suits, and politicians who have been the biggest
obstacles in your community's anti–drug-abuse efforts made
as public as possible. And finally, you want the success of
your group's activities published far and wide, so that other
communities pick up the ball.

Liaison with Other Groups

Your community group must do all in its power to involve itself with other like-minded organizations around the
country, in the spirit of mutual support. It is also in your
interest to do everything in your power to influence the tens
of thousands of community groups already in existence—

[1] Tim Wall, Neighborhood Anti-Crime Center pamphlet, entitled "Getting Justice from the Criminal Justice System." Published by Citizens for
a Greater New York, 3 West 29 Street, New York, New York, 10001.

whose power and influence is being wasted—to turn their efforts against the druggie.

The networking of community organizations should have as its ultimate goal the influencing of our nation's politicians and bureaucrats toward a change of heart and philosophy. If enough local organizations eliminate drugs from their communities by focusing their efforts against the users; a clear message will be sent to our foundering leaders:
Ours is the route to follow.

Voter Power

One of the most powerful weapons a BAD organization has in influencing politicians and obtaining legislation that will make our courts and justice systems a deterrent to drug buyers is the power of the vote. In general, the BAD organization should vote for, support, and even campaign for, all politicians and legislation aimed at making the druggie accountable for his actions and the law a deterrent for the *buying* and *consuming* of illegal drugs. Politicians who support or advocate the following types of legislation, action, and/or programs should be fully supported:

• Any legislation making a person who gives or sells drugs culpable for all damages—deaths, car accidents, and so on—suffered or caused by the person they caused to be intoxicated.

• Any legislation making pregnant druggies responsible both criminally and civilly for the damage inflicted on their unborn fetuses.

• Any legislation for the drug testing of anyone involved in any employment that can affect the public safety or trust.

• Any legislation for mandatory lifetime treatment for druggies involved in crime.

• Any legislation making people whose homes are used (whether it be during a party or any other situation) for the distribution of drugs (whether sold or given free) guilty of constructive possession of the drugs and liable for all damages caused therefrom.

• Any program for the funding of citizens' antidruggie organizations.

• The demilitarization of the war on drugs.

A BAD organization should vote and campaign with all its resources *against* any politician who believes *any* of the following to be true:

• Our drug problem is created by "the availability" of drugs.

• Drugs are the enemy.

• Stopping drugs at the source is the solution.

• More jobs is the solution.

• More treatment on demand (the demand of the druggie) is the solution.

• More money for law enforcement, education, and treatment programs (of the type we have been funding for the past three decades) is the solution.

• Our drug problem is due to a secret foreign effort to undermine our youth by flooding our streets with drugs.

• Military action in other countries is an answer to our drug problem.

• Greater sentences for drug dealers is an answer to our drug problem.

• Our drug problem has been caused by Martian invaders.

God bless us all.

4

Antidruggie Tactics for Suburban and Rural Areas

THE EXPANDING SUBURBAN AND RURAL DRUG MARKET

In recent years street-level drug trafficking in suburbia and small town U.S.A. has increased dramatically. There are three principal reasons for this. *First,* the farther away from urban areas where drug supplies are plentiful, the more profitable the business for an enterprising drug dealer. In Prince William County, Virginia (a suburb of Washington, D.C.), for example, crack dealers get $20 for an amount that would only bring them $5 on the streets of the nation's capital. A "rock" of crack that sold for $50 in the city could be cut into seven or eight pieces selling for $50 each in the suburbs. During the time when an ounce of cocaine sold for between $500 to $700 in New York City, in Rockland County, a suburb eighteen miles to the north, that same ounce could be sold for as much as $3,000.

Drug dealing in the small towns and suburbs of America has become so profitable that even the normally urban drug

gangs are now spreading their operations out into the heart-
lands. There is no greater example of this movement than in
the suburbs surrounding our own nation's capital, where
drug arrests in some of the outer suburbs—stretching from
the Chesapeake Bay to the Shenandoah Valley—have more
than tripled since 1985. Places like the normally placid Wilmington, Delaware, are experiencing gang violence once
thought to be the exclusive domain of big cities like New
York, L.A., or Chicago. Some recent news reports are typical: Wilmington, Delaware, police arrested two New York
City youths and charged them with murder, in what was
described as a "drug-related" shooting that killed one person and left four people injured. Charged with first-degree
murder were two boys, 19 years and 17 years, who were
believed to have brought drugs from New York City to Wilmington to sell.[1] A drug task force in Cabell County, West
Virginia, arrested four suspected drug dealers from
Colombus, Ohio, in a local Holiday Inn with a quantity of
cocaine. "Most of the drugs in the area are being brought in
from Colombus and Detroit," said a local prosecutor.[2]
Crime throughout mostly rural North Carolina jumped a
whopping 10.1 percent in 1989, surpassing the national average, with much of it being attributed to the rise in illegal
drug use.[3]

The conditions are the same from coast to coast. In April
1988 the National League of Cities met to share ideas on
"fighting the spread of crack onto Main Street, U.S.A."
Places like Longmont, Colorado, population 50,000; Sea-
ford, Delaware, population 6,000; Bellevue, Nebraska, pop-

[1] UPI news release 1332, 9/13/90.
[2] UPI news release 1825, 9/16/90.
[3] Cathy Cash, "North Carolina Crime Leaps," UPI news release, 9/17/90.

ulation 32,000; Jefferson City, Missouri, population 36,000; and Palm Springs, California, one of our nation's richest communities, reported having drug problems significant enough to necessitate "big-city actions," such as "hiring undercover police, searching schools for drugs, and trying to teach kids to say no to drugs."[1] A recent General Accounting Office report indicated that rural areas now have arrest rates for drug- and alcohol-related offenses that are "as high as cities'."[2]

Second, many drug dealers believe that they stand a lesser chance of being arrested and have more opportunities to "buy" police protection in areas with small, ill-equipped, unsophisticated, overworked, and underpaid police departments, than in the multiagency urban areas. All you've got to do is check the Associated Press or the United Press wire services on almost any given day and you'll find a story about police corruption, linked to drugs, in a suburban or rural community. Today's offering (UPS 0991, 9/9/90), for example, was from Ellijay, Georgia, where two deputy sheriffs and a county commissioner were arrested and charged with accepting payoffs from drug dealers and running their own methamphetamine lab. One suburban community—Middletown, Connecticut, population 45,000—blamed the rapid increase in its local drug problems on the community's growth in affluence. In 1989 drug arrests zoomed to 277, nearly double the previous year's total; and, according to the chief of police, George R. Aylward, ten of the force's ninety officers "may have been compromised in their duties by contact with drug dealers."[3] Considering the failed route

[1] LaBarbara Bowman, "Small Towns Fight Big City Drugs," *USA Today,* 4/27/88.
[2] Philip Brasher, "Rural Drugs," AP news release, 9/20/90.
[3] Kirk Johnson, "As a City's Wealth Grows, So Does Its Drug Problem," *The New York Times,* 1/12/89.

our leaders persist in following in this alleged drug war, it looks like there will be no end to it.

The third and most important reason for the drug dealers' unstopped migration is that nowhere in America is it more evident by the complaisance of the people that the Big Lie and phony war on drugs have been bought hook line and sinker than in the suburbs and towns of our heartland. For example, as a result of the April 1988 League of Cities meeting, the Congress—at the mayors' urging—declared December 3 through 9 to be "National Cities Fight Back *Against Drugs* Week."[1] It was obvious that suburbia and small town U.S.A.—used to the good life and unaccustomed to questioning government—had joined the war *against drugs,* and not against the users; a war that has been, and will continue to be, doomed to failure. It is also obvious that as long as suburban communities continue to have faith in political slogans and empty promises, and fail to put the fear of the law into their own druggies, their communities will continue to be fertile, beckoning grounds for drug dealers.

Just hearing the phrase *war against drugs* should prickle the hair on the neck of any member of a BAD organization, as it does mine. Had the mayors named that week National Fight Back Against *Drug Abusers* Week, by now we would be a long way toward having solved the drug problem—at least in suburbia and small town U.S.A., where the druggie is most vulnerable. Once again, if our leaders won't aim their efforts in the only direction that can and will win—at controlling the drug consumers—an organized group of citizens must show them the way.

[1] LaBarbara Bowman, "Small Towns Fight Big City Drugs," *USA Today,* 4/27/88.

CREATING A SUBURBAN AND RURAL ENVIRONMENT HOSTILE FOR DRUG SHOPPING

A well-organized and solidly focused citizens' action group will find getting rid of the druggies in suburban and rural areas—in comparison to the big-city battlegrounds—so simply and easily done that people will be left scratching their heads and wondering why they didn't think of it before. The typically open layout of these areas, the lack of the anonymity afforded by the big-city environment; the more inquisitive nature of suburbanites about strangers in their neighborhoods; the fact that most drug buyers must use vehicles on their shopping expeditions; the financial stake people have in their homes and quality of life in their communities, together spell *doom* to the frightened and paranoid druggie.

DEFINITION OF SUBURBAN AND RURAL AREAS

For the tactical purposes of this book *suburban area* is defined as any residential area, either within or outside a city's boundaries, that is typified by single and two-family homes. *Rural areas* are those areas typified by farms, small towns, and large stretches of sparsely populated countryside.

Organization and Equipment

The principles of organization and the equipment requirements discussed earlier in this book are equally applicable in the suburbs, towns, and rural areas. Again, considering the financial stake most people in these areas have in their homes, cooperation and support should not be difficult to obtain. It is something that organizers must stress when contacting members of the community for their support. For example:

"Do you know that drugs are being sold in three locations in our community, and that as long as this is allowed to continue the value of your home is dropping?"

SUBURBAN AND RURAL LAW ENFORCEMENT

In suburbia and small town U.S.A., most of the law-enforcement people, prosecutors, and elected officials whose cooperation you will be trying to get live in and have as much at stake in your community as you do, and will be glad to assist you.

Suburban and Rural Drug-Trafficking Patterns

(Exclusive of drug laboratories and stash houses, which will be discussed separately)

Street-level drug-trafficking patterns in suburban and rural areas are almost impossible to hide or disguise. Unlike an urban environment, with both buyer and dealer camouflaged by the helter-skelter of big-city life and protected by a system of law that demands clear, unmistakable observations on the part of surveilling law-enforcement officers, suburban dealers and buyers must do their thing virtually out in the open.

Drug dealing in these areas usually follows one of two distinct patterns; the first is a house or series of houses, from where drug dealers sell their wares, usually called a "drug den," or "crack house." The second is the use of known street locations—or any outdoor area—where dealers loiter on foot or in cars waiting for the arrival of customers; these are called "open-air drug markets." The vast majority of druggies in either situation arrive by car, making them sitting ducks—and they know it. It's up to the local BAD organization to remind them of it.

Here again, as in urban areas, the discussion of antidruggie actions is separated into three categories: **Visible Threat, Tactical Street Action,** and **Strategic Action.**

THE VISIBLE THREAT IN SUBURBIA

Nowadays it is hard to find a suburban or rural school district that does not have DRUG-FREE SCHOOL ZONE signs posted around it. What the presence of these signs tell me is, first, that there is a drug problem serious enough to merit their being posted; second, that the people who posted the signs—while well meaning—do not understand the resilience of a drug-abuse problem, unless directly and unmistakably attacked *at the user level.* And while the size of the signs (most are about three feet square and bigger), their visibility (large blue or black letters on a white background), and the permanent nature of their posting (on steel poles embedded in concrete, or in heavy steel sign frames) are ideal for the purpose of a visible threat, the message—as usual, intended to frighten drug dealers—threatens no one. They have no measurable effect whatsoever on local drug trafficking.

These signs are generally posted around schools, as a reflection of the recent federal law making the sale of drugs within a thousand feet of a school punishable by more than fifty years in prison. Having led one of the first enforcement actions utilizing this law (discussed earlier in this book; "Anatomy of a Failure"), I think I'm pretty well qualified in restating how futile it—or any law aimed at the dealer, no matter how Draconian the punishment—is in achieving a drug-free *anything*.

I remember making an undercover meet with a drug dealer a few blocks from a school. I had lured him there to make sure that when we arrested him he would be charged with the stiffer crime. We sat parked under one of these signs discussing prices. I was playing my undercover role to the hilt, haggling like crazy over the price of a couple of kilos of cocaine, when the dealer suddenly looked up at the sign, laughed, and said, "Hey man, we in a drug-*free* zone. I guess I ain't suppos' to be chargin' you *any* money."

One small town, Columbus, Nebraska, caught up in the drug-free-school-zone, War-on-Drugs hype, adopted a city resolution establishing a drug-free zone "anywhere youth are found." This included public swimming pools, video arcade centers, youth centers, playgrounds, and even "private youth centers." Without realizing it the Columbus City Council, because of the geographical placement of these areas, had made the whole city a drug-free zone, without ever mentioning the drug user.[1]

The Circle of Fear

Unlike in big cities, where an unknowable number of drug-dealing locations may be hidden in heavily populated areas running for miles in any direction, in suburban and rural communities one can often take a map of the area and put an X on *all* suspect locations. This makes the dealers

[1] "Columbus Becomes Drug-Free Zone," UPI news release 2215, 9/17/90.

vulnerable to what I call a "Circle of Fear" stranglehold on their life's-blood flow of customers. A circle is drawn around each X, or cluster of X's, representing an area of about a quarter to a half mile in diameter, completely surrounding the suspect location(s). If some of the locations are more than a half mile distant from each other, separate circles must be calculated, attacking each area as a separate problem.

The Circle of Fear is the area through which the druggie must pass on the way to his supplier—an area that must be made so visibly hostile that his need for drugs is replaced with paranoid panic. From the moment he enters the area he must feel like a cockroach on a white linoleum floor in broad daylight, with the stomping heel of the community somewhere above him.

The main advantage offered by the concept is the avoidance of direct confrontation with dealers. A well-planned and -executed Circle of Fear is something no dealer can fight. He is simply starved into moving to a more hospitable community.

You can then erase your X.

The Wandering Drug Dealer

Usually the next question I get is, Isn't the drug dealer just going to just move to another location, perhaps another community? And my answer is: Yes, just as long as it isn't in *your* community.

Unfortunately—until the many years of *drug war* media hype can be overcome—a community's attitude must be selfish and short-focused. Too many of your neighboring communities are going to remain mired in the belief that a *war on drugs* and not the *druggie,* is still the answer and that the drug problem is one the police, the military, the CIA—and whomever else some harebrained politician succeeds in throwing into the fray—can handle on their own. Unfortunately, at the beginning of your campaign, you must let them pay the price for that folly.

All BAD organizations must do everything possible to convince neighboring communities to join with them in their efforts; but they must do so without ever losing sight of the fact that their first concern *must* be their own community. In the end your efforts will be doing more for the winning of an overall drug war than all the hundreds of billions of taxpayer dollars wasted to date. The success in your community will be contagious. Once other towns and communities have seen how easily you were able to rid yourself of a street-dealing problem, they will soon follow suit.

Besides, most drug-enforcement professionals agree that keeping dealers on the move has a definite disruptive and lessening effect on overall drug-trafficking levels. Dealers must remain in locations that their customers know, and where they feel relatively safe about coming. Each BAD organization's goal must be to make sure that *that* location does not exist in *their* community.

Posting the Circle of Fear

Since the suburban drug-buyer almost always travels by car he is more vulnerable to the effects of sign posting than his urban brother. In this section I will recommend a variety of warning messages; however, *no single type should be relied on exclusively.*

As a druggie moves into and through a Circle of Fear he should see a variety of warnings. At the outskirts of the

town or community he should see a large *angry* billboard
that might read:

DRUG BUYERS BEWARE!
YOU ARE NOW ENTERING A COMMUNITY THAT
WILL NOT TOLERATE YOUR PRESENCE.
STOP HERE TO BUY SOME DRUGS AND
WE'LL MAKE SURE YOU ALSO BUY SOME TIME.

The streets and roads approaching suspect locations—
within the Circle of Fear—must be posted with the same
(physical) types of signs used around schools; however—
unlike the drug-free school zone signs—the BAD threat
must be *clear* and *unequivocal.* I recommend two or three
different types of warnings posted on each block. A community should select those messages that can best be backed up
with action, if need be. Some examples might be:

WARNING TO DRUG BUYERS!
THIS HAS BEEN IDENTIFIED AS A
DRUG-DEALING LOCATION AND IS BEING
OBSERVED BY A CITIZENS' PATROL GROUP IN
RADIO CONTACT WITH POLICE PATROLS. DRUG
BUYERS WILL BE ARRESTED AND PROSECUTED.

An alternate sign on the same street might read:

DRUG BUYERS BEWARE!
HIDDEN SURVEILLANCE CAMERAS ARE
PHOTOGRAPHING ALL THOSE IN THIS AREA
WHO ARE SUSPECTED OF BUYING DRUGS.
PHOTOS AND LICENSE PLATE NUMBERS ARE
TURNED OVER TO THE POLICE AND
DRUG-ENFORCEMENT ADMINISTRATION.

Or the more simple:

DRUG BUYERS BEWARE!
THIS AREA UNDER SURVEILLANCE.
YOU MAY BE STOPPED AND ARRESTED AS
YOU LEAVE THIS AREA WITH YOUR DRUGS.

One of the biggest weapons the suburban or rural BAD organization has against the druggie invading their turf is the Controlled Substances Act, as amended, May 1, 1987. Paragraph (a) (4) reads:

> (a) The following shall be subject to forfeiture to the United States and no property right shall exist in them: . . . (4) All conveyances, including aircraft, vehicles, or vessels, which are used, or are intended for use, to transport, or in any manner to facilitate the transportation, sale, receipt, possession, or concealment of [illegal drugs].

This means very simply that anyone using a car to buy drugs is subject to *immediately* losing it. There are no ifs, ands, or buts about it. If illegal drugs—in any amount—are found in someone's car, they can kiss it good-bye. And the real beauty of the law is that the seizure of the car is a separate legal proceeding from the druggie's case in court. It's called an *in rem* (against the object) proceeding, which means that the car is seized whether or not the druggie is found guilty, or even arrested. Therefore, one of the primary fears we want to exploit—in addition to the fear of arrest and exposure—is the immediate loss of the druggie's car; a very significant loss in suburbia and rural America, where the car is vital. Thus, another sign along the drug-buying route might read:

DRUGGIES BEWARE!
YOU WILL LOSE YOUR CAR AS WELL AS YOUR FREEDOM. SUSPECTED DRUG-DEALING LOCATIONS ARE UNDER SURVEILLANCE—ALL VEHICLES USED TO VIOLATE THE DRUG LAWS ARE SUBJECT TO IMMEDIATE SEIZURE AND FORFEITURE.

The signs, once again, are only limited by the group's imagination. They should be posted in such a way that each and every one is impossible to miss and easy to read. I recommend that temporary signs of paint and cardboard be posted and checked for ease of visibility and effect by members of the group driving through the area at different speeds before permanent ones are installed.

The psychological edge that suburban and rural sign-posting has over urban, and why the tactic must be emphasized and exploited to its fullest, is that—due to the open, exposed, and less populated nature of the areas involved—the visible threat of a properly worded and posted sign touches the druggie's paranoia button a lot more directly. When a sign refers to a "suspected drug-dealing location" or "locations under surveillance," how many can there be? You're not dealing with row after row of buildings with thousands of possible locations for drug dealers on a single block. The average druggie will *know* that his dealer is being watched and move on.

Street Sellers in Suburbia

The other pattern of suburban and rural drug-dealing being used with increasing frequency is the open-air drug market. Groups of dealers on foot—with stashes of drugs concealed in nearby homes, cars, tree stumps, or other hiding places—loiter in a fixed area well known to local druggies and service a flow of customers on the open street. The open-air market might be anything from one intersection to several square blocks around a small housing development or park.

From a logistical point of view an entire suspect area should be treated as though it were one big drug-dealing house. The Circle of Fear should be drawn around the entire area so that those approaching it from any direction must pass from four to six city blocks (or a quarter of a mile), posted with signs, before entering the area itself.

In recent years small-town and suburban police have become increasingly sophisticated in their methods of enforcing the drug laws, and out of frustration with conventional enforcement methods—and in spite of criticism against them—have instituted reverse undercover operations, targeting the drug buyers. Undercover police officers posing as street dealers sell drugs to unwary customers who are then arrested. I will discuss the use of this type of law-enforcement operation in suburban and rural settings a little further on in this section, but for the purposes of posting Visible Threat signs, don't forget to mention it:

DRUGGIES BEWARE!
YOU MAY BE BUYING DRUGS FROM A NARC.
THE AREA YOU ARE ENTERING IS A KNOWN
DRUG-DEALING AREA. UNDERCOVER OFFICERS
ARE POSING AS DRUG DEALERS. YOU ARE
SUBJECT TO ARREST AND IMPRISONMENT FOR
BUYING DRUGS.

Druggies are not a courageous lot. If they were, they'd be facing life instead of hiding from it with chemicals. A well-planned and -executed Circle of Fear around any suburban or rural drug-dealing location will reap an immediate and drastic reduction in the level of trafficking, and in most instances will totally eliminate it. But like any good job of fumigating, after you've eliminated the infestation, you want to make double sure it doesn't return.

Floodlighting

The unnerving effect of sign posting will be made doubly effective by floodlighting all suspected drug-dealing areas—the brighter the better. Whenever you encounter a situation where it seems too confrontational with the dealers inside a drug den or crack house to focus floodlights directly on *it,* then floodlight the whole block. Make certain that arriving druggies *know* that people behind windows are writing down their license-plate numbers and possibly videotaping them—even at night. Another possible sign to be posted near suspect locations might be:

WARNING TO DRUGGIES!
THIS AREA FLOODLIGHTED TO
ENABLE THE VIDEOTAPING OF
DRUG TRANSACTIONS AND
THE POSITIVE IDENTIFICATION OF
DRUG BUYERS.

Floodlights combined with this type of sign should also be very effective in open-air drug market locations.

SUBURBAN STREET TACTICS

Suburban and rural street tactics vary from the urban, primarily in that the open spaces, lower density of population, and use of vehicles by drug buyers will necessitate more of an emphasis on surveillance and the use of patrol vehicles, as opposed to foot-patrol activities.

That is not to say that the foot patrol is ruled out.

Every situation is different and somewhat unpredictable, and should be met with all the resources and imagination at your group's disposal. *Every* tactic, technique, and idea described in this book may be useful in an urban, suburban, and/or rural setting. The only rule that must always be kept in mind is that the target of *all* activities is the *druggie,* and *not* the drug dealer. Leave the dealer to the police and, please—no matter what kind of area you live in—read the *whole* book.

Suburban Foot Patrols

Community foot patrols in the more populated suburban areas should follow all the suggestions listed earlier in this book. In those communities where the drug dealing occurs in isolated and identifiable locations, a foot patrol might—after you've already created and posted a Circle of Fear—seem like overkill. But in a campaign dedicated to "convincing" druggies that a community is a BAD one to buy drugs in, no legal measure can be considered overkill. So if your group feels foot patrols might be helpful . . . *use them!*

One of the most dangerous, drug-infested areas of our nation is Washington, D.C., which, at this writing, is experiencing a record-breaking year in drug-related murders,

along with every other crime linked to drugs.[1] While techni-
cally—if measured by density of population and general living conditions—Washington, D.C., is as urban and inner-
city as you can get, many of its neighborhoods are suburban
in construction and physical layout.

One such neighborhood—the tough, drug-and-crime-in-
fested Anacostia—is patrolled on foot by a citizens' organization known as the Fairlawn Coalition, wearing *bright or-
ange baseball caps* and armed with nothing more than
radios, video cameras, and binoculars. The group confronts
drug dealers *and users* with stares instead of verbal or physical confrontation. According to the group's founder, John
Foreman, "They have driven the *buyers* out."[2]

They are among the very few groups who have recognized that their success—in spite of the fact that they also
confront drug dealers, which I do *not* recommend—is
mainly due to "frightening the buyers away." If the Fairlawn Coalition could do it in Washington, D.C.—one of the
most dangerous cities in our nation—*it can be done anywhere.* Unfortunately, groups like this are rare.

One of the main purposes of this book is to change that.

Vehicle Patrol

As I recommended earlier in this book, all vehicles used
for community patrol work—vans, cars, trucks, et cetera—
should be plainly marked, so that just their obvious and
well-manned presence enhances the Circle of Fear effect by
lending credence to the threat of the group to back up its

[1] "President Bush Says Drugs Remain His Top Concern," UPI news release 1619, 9/5/90.
[2] Carolyn Skorneck, "Drug War—Individuals," AP news release,
12/26/89.

warning signs. Three men in a well-marked community patrol vehicle, with field glasses and obvious radio equipment, parked along an approach route to a known drug-dealing location within a well-posted Circle of Fear would prevent any druggie that I've ever known from ever driving down that road again, not to mention stopping to make a buy. And you can bet the word would travel quickly among the area druggies.

Vehicle Equipment

The equipment requirements for the suburban patrol vehicle are the same as for its urban counterpart—a revolving emergency bubble-light,[1] flashlights, side-mounted floodlights, binoculars, bullhorn or loudspeaker system, camera (video camera is preferable), and of utmost importance: radio communication equipment.

Radio Communications

In the suburbs and rural areas—where there are fewer police on patrol with longer distances to cover—being in radio contact with local police is extremely important. Thus, before going on patrol, the group must arrange—with either the local police, sheriff's department, or state police —either to obtain one of their radios, or have the police monitor the group's activities on a CB radio. Many suburban and rural police departments already have CB monitors; however, if they don't, it may be necessary for your organization to provide them with one.

---

[1] Check with local police in each suburban area for what color emergency light may be used. You do not want to be confused with a volunteer fire brigade.

At the very least, community patrol vehicles must be in radio contact with someone near a phone, who can contact the police for them. A sign on the side of your community patrol vehicle reading THIS VEHICLE IN RADIO COMMUNICATION WITH POLICE will both frighten the pants off perspective drug-buyers and garner the respect of local dealers.

Use of Cameras and Bullhorns in Patrol Vehicle

(DRIVE-BY TECHNIQUE)

The open and exposed nature of drug trafficking in suburbia and rural areas makes the use of cameras in a roving patrol an extremely potent psychological weapon against the paranoid druggie. By the time a potential drug-buyer has passed through a Circle of Fear and stops his car to make a buy, he will no doubt be concerned about the vulnerability of his position. Unlike the urban setting with its teeming streets, where the druggie can fool himself into believing, *Hell, they can't prove anything. There's a million people on the street,* the suburban or rural druggie finds himself either a lone, exposed target parking in front of a drug den, or a sitting duck on an open street, where the only people on foot are either drug dealers or undercover narcs.

If at that moment a bright red, well-marked patrol vehicle drives slowly by, with someone pointing a video camera at him, you can imagine his reaction.

The bullhorn, in suburban and rural settings, may be used in a direct, focused manner on the usually car-borne druggies. For example, say Third and Main streets is the known drug-connection spot in your town and, nine times out of ten, cars stopped in the vicinity with occupants inside are druggies looking for a connection. Now your motor patrol spots such a car parked with its motor running. The street is so floodlit that it looks like daylight. You can see him nervously craning around in his seat looking for his connection, who may have already left the area due to a sudden decline in business. Somehow this druggie has braved your Circle of Fear, passing signs that told him that he was being observed and filmed; that he might be buying drugs from an undercover narc; that his license number, photo, and description were being turned over to the police; and that—at best—he would lose his car, *if* he stopped to buy drugs. You can bet, at that moment, he is a very nervous druggie.

Suddenly, a well-marked BAD patrol vehicle cruises by; a camera is pointed in the druggie's direction; a voice blasts at him over a bullhorn—"YOU ARE IN A DRUG-DEALING ZONE! ALL PEOPLE WHO STOP HERE ARE FILMED! AT THIS MOMENT WE ARE RADIOING YOUR DESCRIPTION AND LICENSE NUMBER TO STATE AND LOCAL POLICE!"

What do you think he will do now?

Even in the toughest of urban settings there are few druggies who could withstand this type of attack without having a serious nerve-and-bodily-function crisis. In the suburbs or rural areas, where there are no buildings, crowds, or traffic to disappear into, you'll rarely have to complete a full sentence before the only trace of a druggie is his exhaust fumes.

Installation of Loudspeakers, Floodlights, and Video Cameras.

In some situations drive-by techniques may bring too much potential for dealer confrontation. In these cases the group must focus their efforts on the semipermanent or permanent installation of loudspeakers, floodlights, and video cameras, concentrating them on the drug-dealing location. The loudspeakers (as described earlier) should be of a type

that can be operated from a hidden location—a car, a mobile van, or some hidden OP. The same techniques I described earlier may be used in the suburban setting as well.

VIDEO CAMERAS

The use of video cameras may become an important legal
weapon as well as a tactical one. Recently, in Hempstead,
Long Island, a suburb of New York City, an undercover
police operation aimed at street sellers on Terrace Avenue,
"known for crack and cocaine pushers," made heavy use of
video-camera recordings of the sales. The trafficking pattern
was typical of a suburban open-air market.

Nassau County Assistant District Attorney Joseph Burruano described the dealers as "street-level dealers . . . responsible for bringing the drugs into Nassau County from
New York City." Undercover officers made buys from street
dealers who were later arrested. Hempstead Village Mayor
James Garner was later quoted as saying that the operation
was "sending a message that it will be a real tough business
in terms of selling drugs in our village,"[1] emphasizing, once
again, the get-the-dealer fixation of most politicians. But the
operation's use of videotaped evidence did offer suburban
and rural BAD organizations a possible new legal weapon.

"We have very good videotapes [of the buys]," said
Hempstead Assistant District Attorney Burruano, "and
based on this evidence we expect many of those arrested will
plead guilty."[2]

The suggestion is clear. If the dealers can be forced to
plead guilty on the result of videotaped evidence, why not

[1] Henry G. Logeman, "Limos Used to Gut Hempstead Crack Trade,"
UPI news release 1423, 9/13/90.
[2] *Ibid.*

the buyers too? If there were a BAD organization in Hempstead, one of the first steps it would have taken—after the police operation—would have been to capitalize on the publicity surrounding the raids, and tack up signs in the raided area, saying:

DRUG BUYERS BEWARE!
ALL DRUG BUYS ARE BEING VIDEOTAPED.
SUCH *EVIDENCE* MAY BE ENOUGH TO
CONVICT YOU OF FEDERAL AND STATE
FELONY DRUG *POSSESSION* CHARGES!

How to Back Up Your Threats with Police Action

Community organizations in suburban and rural areas have an advantage over their urban counterparts in obtaining prompt police action, simply because most law enforcement officials and prosecutors—sheriffs, district and county attorneys, and chiefs of police—are either elected officials and local residents themselves, or they are appointed by local officials who were elected by a relatively small electorate. A lot more attention is paid to the individual vote in rural and suburban America than in urban areas. Thus political clout—the number of votes your organization represents—is a potent tool in obtaining *druggie-oriented* police actions. But you've got to know what you want.

It is important, when approaching law-enforcement officials, to be specific and clear about the types of police action your organization wants. Being knowledgeable about the kind of problem you have and how you want it addressed by local police will get their immediate attention and the kind of action you want. Being vague—*We've got drug dealers on the corner of Fifth and Main; do something about it!*—will result in more dealer-oriented operations, turnstile justice, and the prolongation of your community's problems.

DRUGGIE-ORIENTED POLICE ACTIONS

The three types of police actions your group should request are **Reverse Undercover** operations, **Angeling-Off** operations, and **Car-Seizure** operations. These are druggie-oriented law-enforcement techniques that will make the threats posted in a Circle of Fear both real and effective. There are two other types of police actions, the employment of which may be considered for the more severe, well-entrenched problems—**Cul-de-Sac** operation and **Shadowing** operation.

THE SUBURBAN REVERSE UNDERCOVER OPERATION

This type of undercover operation (described earlier), involving undercover agents posing as dealers who sell drugs and then arrest the buyers, is particularly effective in the suburban open-air drug markets. In Florida last year, for example, a statewide "crack crackdown," coordinated by the Florida State Sheriff's Association, combined reverse undercover techniques and "Trojan horse" operations with remarkable success in the temporary stoppage of suburban street dealing.[1]

In Mount Clemens, Michigan, a suburb of Detroit, police posing as crack dealers arrested and seized the cars of any would-be customers who drove up looking for drugs. According to an Associated Press release the Mount Clemens operation was believed to be the first of its type in the Detroit area. "Lieutenant Brian Krutell said that twenty-one

[1] Patrick Reyna, AP news release 1601, 8/26/89.

people had been arrested and nine cars seized in a north-east-side neighborhood plagued with street dealing and drug-related violence."[1]

The officers had merely loitered in an area known as an open-air drug supermarket and arrested anyone who "pulled up to the curb and asked for drugs." The operation was carried out under the strict guidelines of Macomb County Prosecutor Carl Marlinga and the drug buys were videotaped by police hiding in a nearby van. The police ended up by seizing, under the Michigan Drug Forfeiture Law, $22,000 in property from the drug customers, including nine vehicles, cash, and jewelry.

I recently spoke with Minneapolis police lieutenant Tom Sawina, who had just completed a successful reverse undercover operation in a Minneapolis suburb. Lieutenant Sawina echoed the sentiments of almost every narcotics enforcement officer I've ever spoken to, in praise of the effectiveness of reverse undercover operations in quickly upsetting drug-trafficking patterns in a given area, by frightening the buyers away.

ANGELING-OFF OPERATION

I don't know how the term *angeling off* got started. I first heard it from an old-time New York City narc, whom I was working with, in the mid 1960s, years during which plainclothes cops in the Big Apple had to maintain a quota of drug arrests. "You get a drug-dealing location," he explained. "You sit on it [observe it]. When you see a customer come out you follow him a couple of blocks and bust him. So anytime you need a dope collar [arrest] you got

[1] AP news release 0548, 12/07/89.

one. . . . But," he cautioned, "you got to be real careful not to burn the location or they'll shut down and move."

Isn't that what we want?

The suburban drug buyer is far more vulnerable to be angeled off than the urban druggie, who can quickly dissolve in a heavy flow of pedestrian traffic. To take advantage of this vulnerability and to show local drug buyers that the posted signs are more than mere threats, the community BAD organization should videotape those few locations and sellers who have still managed to stay in business—despite the Circle of Fear and other tactics described in these pages —and turn the tapes over to the police, along with the request for an *angeling-off* operation.

You WANT as many druggies arrested as possible, *before* the dealer is arrested. You WANT the local druggies to know, beyond any doubt, that your community is a BAD one in which to go drug shopping, and that the signs they see in the Circle of Fear are promises—not empty threats.

CAR-SEIZURE OPERATIONS

A key card a BAD organization can play in convincing suburban or rural police to conduct a car-seizure operation is the fact that, under federal law—if there is no state law enabling authorities to seize drug buyers' vehicles—not only can the local police seize a drug buyer's car, but they can keep it for their own official use, or sell it at auction and use the proceeds for their own drug-war expenses.

In contacting your local police you might point out that other suburban departments, like the Mount Clemens, Michigan, police (example cited in "Reverse Undercover" section), are already taking advantage of laws permitting the seizure of drug buyers' assets, and that if they have any questions they can contact the nearest Drug Enforcement

Administration office or United States attorney's office, for specific instructions.

A car-seizure operation functions pretty much the same as an angeling-off operation, with additional provisions made by police for the immediate seizure and impounding of drug buyers' cars. This will necessitate extra manpower to handle the cars and the paperwork involved.

But it will be worth it!

The police lie in ambush at the outer limits of the Circle of Fear. They are radioed descriptions of drug buyers, their vehicles, and the routes they take after leaving the scene of a purchase. Just when the druggie thinks he is home free he is stopped, searched, and, when the drugs are found, arrested; and his car seized. Thus the buyer—whether or not you can convince local judges and district attorneys to prosecute him—will at least pay the penalty of losing his car. From time to time a druggie will be spotted making a buy, yet when he is stopped and "tossed" no drugs are found. In all likelihood he has swallowed the evidence or sensed he was going to be stopped and threw it out the window. Even though he must be released, you can bet that neither he, nor any other druggie he knows, will ever return to your community.

So, go get em!

AUGMENTING POLICE

In suburban and rural areas police departments may be too undermanned and ill equipped to carry out any kind of antidruggie operations. To augment the police the BAD organization should volunteer its patrol members to identify buyers and their descriptions via hidden OPs and CB or police radio, leaving the police extra manpower to make arrests and seize cars. The organization should also then be prepared to testify in court if need be.

AN EXAMPLE OF A POLICE-RUN CIRCLE OF FEAR ("OPERATION CUL-DE-SAC")

Thanks to the crack explosion many areas on the outskirts of some of our cities, which once might have been described as suburban, have become virtual war zones. Newton, a Los Angeles community that was once, according to resident Sang Brown, "the sort of place where people had pride in their homes and beautiful lawns," is one such area. Last year, when Los Angeles had 873 homicides, 100 of them happened in Newton. The Los Angeles Police Department decided to take drastic action—the kind of action that some of our harder-hit communities around the country might want to consider. They called it "Operation Cul-de-Sac."

The police cordoned off the Newton community—thirty square blocks —with concrete barricades and off-limit signs, declaring "NARCOTICS ENFORCEMENT AREA, OPEN TO RESIDENTS ONLY." Uniformed police manned the barricades and checked incoming cars for "gang-bangers." The term *residents only* was "meaningless," according to Captain Gordon Harrison, commanding officer for Newton. He said it was a "psychological barrier." Few arrests were made, yet within six weeks violent crime fell nearly ninety percent. Civil libertarians were up in arms, but 558 of 563 Newton residents polled approved of the action.[1]

What the police had done, whether they realized it or not,

[1] Eloise Salholz with Mark Miller and Lynda Wright, "The 'Walled Cities' of L.A.," *Newsweek*, 5/14/90.

was apply so much heat to the area, the drug buyers looked elsewhere. And once they left, so did violent crime.

SHADOWING OPERATION

Wherever uniformed police are, drug buyers refuse to go. Charleston, South Carolina, Police Chief Reuban Greenberg recognized this years ago, when, after countless futile roundups of drug dealers, he decided that, instead of arresting them, he would treat them as small businessmen and simply disrupt their businesses. The chief assigned uniformed policemen to station themselves several feet away from street dealers and "obviously" shadow them. As a result of the operation the Charleston police noted some very important results:

- Buyers would not approach dealers while police watched them.
- Dealers were restricted to a small walking area because their customers had to know where to find them.
- The dealer did not have to be shadowed all the time because most of his business takes place between the hours of 4:30 P.M. and 3:30 A.M.
- The department did not have to shadow a dealer every day, just a couple of days a week—enough days to make the business unprofitable.

According to the FBI's statistics Charleston's overall crime index dropped thirty-one percent between the years 1982 and 1987—the first five years of the shadowing operation.[1]

[1] Laurent Belsie, "South Carolina Uses New Approach to Fight Drugs," *The Christian Science Monitor*, 8/11/89.

While this type of police action may not be feasible in some of the larger urban areas, it can be employed almost everywhere else. And with a vigilant community organization ready to assist the police no drug dealer's business can survive for long.[1]

RECLAIMING A DRUG ZONE

Even if a community organization fails to convince local authorities to mount antidruggie operations, *any* type of periodic police action will do. As has already been shown, the "heat" generated by the mere presence of police will frighten buyers away. Historically, the problem in permanently ridding communities of drug dealers—urban, suburban, and rural—has always been the absence of heat, *after* the police leave.

"After you guys leave, within a day or so the dealers are back again" are words I've heard thousands of times after just as many drug raids. Of course the dealers return. Because the druggies are already waiting for them with fists full of dollars.

And that's where a BAD organization comes in. Its presence in a community is the personification of *heat.* After a police action temporarily reclaims an area, the BAD organization moves in—with its signs, uniformed patrols, cameras, and bullhorns—and makes the place a druggie-free zone.

Case closed!

---

[1] "Operation Pressure Point" is a variation of this approach, used effectively in some sections of New York City.

Shopping Malls

In talking to drug-enforcement authorities around the nation I have yet to find one who considers shopping malls a drug-*trafficking* problem. However, in many communities they do represent a problem in that video arcades and similar businesses located on the malls seem to attract many teenaged and preteen "heads"—young drug users who are high on drugs and who give and/or sell the stuff to one another. While this is not a real street trafficking problem and comes more under the heading of how each of us handles our children, the existence of one of these places— where drug use is the main attraction—should not be tolerated.

The solution is a simple one. Where parental or official authority is present, drug abuse is not. If there is a troublesome mall location in your community, members of the BAD organization should be regularly posted as observers. This is another area where an attempt should be made to get local youth to police themselves. If after-school hours teams of youngsters are assigned to local malls as uniformed "antidruggie observers," representing either school or community authority—or if any other imaginative variation of this tactic is employed—there will be no problem.

How to Help the Police to Hurt the *Big Dealers* in Suburban and Rural Areas

While I don't endorse the two decades of failed supply-side drug war by itself, I do believe that a concerted effort on the part of our private citizenry in attacking demand, as described in this book, will make these huge, previously meaningless, drug seizures devastatingly effective. And at the present time, nowhere are our citizens in a better position to lend a hand in locating labs and major drug stashes than in suburban and rural America.

Major drug cartels and other criminal organizations have been increasingly turning to rural and suburban communities to hide drug laboratories and to conceal huge drug stashes. In fact, most of the record-breaking drug seizures made during the past four years have been made in rural or suburban areas, and some of them as a result of actions taken by alert private citizens.

As an example of this trend, on September 29, 1989, the biggest drug seizure in history—more than twenty metric tons of cocaine—was made in a warehouse in Sylmar, Los Angeles's northernmost suburb.[1] Records were also found indicating that approximately 132,000 pounds of cocaine had been distributed through the very same warehouse during the two prior years. Before this mammoth event the largest drug seizure on record was an 8,000-pound cocaine grab made in suburban Ft. Lauderdale, Florida, in November 1987. And—as if further proof of this pattern were needed—five days after the Sylmar grab nine tons of cocaine (world's second largest seizure) was taken in a rural home in Harlingen, Texas. Authorities said that the house, surrounded by a citrus grove, was literally "stuffed with cocaine."[2]

"I've been on this job for twenty-five years, and I've never seen so much dope in one place," said John Zienter, special agent in charge of DEA's Los Angeles office, entrusted with the investigation of the Sylmar seizure. "I couldn't believe

[1] E. Scott Reckard, "Cocaine Seizure," AP news release 1010, 9/30/90.
[2] "14 Tons of Cocaine Are Seized in Texas and at Sea," *The New York Times,* 10/6/89.

it."[1] Incredibly, no law-enforcement authority could claim credit for the biggest seizure in the history of the drug war —it came as the result of an alert local resident seeing "suspicious activities in the area" and tipping off police.[2]

What this shows is that the alertness, resourcefulness, and willingness to get involved of our private citizens, besides being the strongest deterrent to drug demand, is also the most powerful unused weapon we have to hurt the dealers where it hurts them the most: in the pocketbook. The Sylmar seizure had an estimated street value of $20 billion and its discovery had nothing to do with any law-enforcement efforts whatsoever. The sheer size of the seizure— more than double the total amount of drugs *all* DEA had seized during the prior year—seemed to indicate that increasing the role of private citizens in certain areas of the law-enforcement war on drugs should have a *higher* priority than increasing the budgets for any of our drug-war bureaucracies.

And the Sylmar seizure was no fluke. Many of our biggest drug seizures have resulted from nothing more than tips by concerned citizens. The difficulty in measuring the amount and significance of this contribution is that the drug-war bureaucracies usually—and I have often been a witness to this—claim the seizures resulted from their efforts, coupling these claims with pleas for bigger budgets. For example, the first report from Sylmar was that the seizure came as the result of a year-long undercover investigation by DEA, and *it* was coupled with a plea for more funding.

The effect of this type of misinformation on our overall

[1] Jay Mathews, "20 Metric Tons of Cocaine, $10 Million Seized; Tip and Two-Day Probe Lead to Record Haul in Los Angeles," *Washington Post,* 9/30/89.
[2] Valerie Kuklenski, "Single Lock Guarded 20-Ton Cocaine Cache," UPI news release 1744, 9/30/89.

approach to ending this drug problem once and for all is that it obfuscates the direction we should now be emphasizing—the full and active participation of the American people.

I want to stress that I am *not* advocating that private citizens conduct drug-trafficking investigations. What I am recommending is that all residents of suburban and rural areas be alerted to certain signs that *may* indicate the presence of either a large drug stash or an illegal laboratory; and that should any of these signs be observed, the local police and/or DEA be notified immediately.

Under no circumstances should a community action group, or any civilian, take any police action in these situations.

Signs That May Indicate the Presence of a Drug Stash or Laboratory in Suburban or Rural Areas

1. Truck, camper (or any other large storage-type vehicle) traffic in unlikely areas.

2. Warehouse activity during other than normal business hours.

3. Use of warehouses and large storage facilities with no company names or advertising posted; or company names that seem suspicious or offbeat.

4. Odd-hour traffic of any kind; vehicles with out-of-state license plates and/or rental cars.

5. People frequenting a warehouse, neighborhood, or any other location who don't seem to "fit"; possibly, too well dressed and sporting jewelry a bit too rich for the area.

6. Abnormally frequent and/or heavy deliveries to a local residence or any other type of structure or location that seems inappropriate.

7. Strange chemical odors emanating from any unlikely

place. **IMPORTANT NOTE:** Illegal drug labs are highly volatile and explode easily.

8. Farms that suddenly seem to have odd, inappropriate vehicular traffic; particularly at odd hours of the night.

9. Unusual security measures like guard dogs, surveillance cameras, and sophisticated alarm systems.

10. Sound of large exhaust fans whirring through the night.

11. Unusually large consumption of gas and electricity (for community members who work in public utility jobs).

Actions You May Take:

1. *Write down:* car descriptions (including license-plate numbers); physical descriptions of people (height, weight, race, age, facial hair, scars, et cetera); times of arrival and departure; times when odors are strongest and direction they appear to be coming from; and any other pertinent facts that you may know about a suspect location.

2. You *might* try to get a phone number of a location that appears suspect by calling telephone-company information services. These are investigative measures that should normally be carried out by police; however, you would be surprised at how often they are simply not done. A heavily trafficked location, a home with no phone, or what appears to be a business with an unlisted phone number should be considered extremely suspicious.

3. Once you have all the information you can obtain without overtly investigating the location and exposing yourself, telephone the local police, *and* the nearest Drug Enforcement Administration office. In the case of a suspected clandestine lab, also notify your local fire department.

* * *

IMPORTANT NOTE: **I recommend that the telephone calls be made anonymously. You are now dealing with high-level drug traffickers—not druggies.**

A True-Life Example

On the afternoon of May 14, 1986, one of the guys in my group—Group 22, DEA's New York Field Division—knocked on my office door.

"Boss," he said, "we just got an anonymous call. A guy out in the ass end of Queens—Little Neck Parkway. It sounds to me like a lab." I knew the area well. I had lived not too far from Little Neck Parkway for several years. It was a suburban community made up of one- and two-family residences, within several blocks of the line separating New York City and Nassau County, Long Island; a predominantly middle- to upper-income Jewish-Italian-Irish community; and about as unlikely an area for a drug lab as you could pick—or so I thought.

"What do you have?"

"The guy said he's seen a lot of Spanish-speaking people coming and going at all hours of the day and night. Most of the cars have out-of-state plates; mostly from Florida. They also have two big Dobermans that seem to be attack trained. The same guy walks them all the time. He had to hold the dogs back once; his jacket flew open and our guy saw a gun in his belt. The caller wrote down one of the Florida license plates. I checked it through Miami and it comes back to a known coke dealer. The guy also saw them bringing in what he said looked like tins of chemicals; and get this: He snooped around and said that the basement windows were all papered over."

I sent a couple of agents out to check out the information

in person. Within a couple of days we verified everything the caller had said and had enough PC for a search warrant.

On May 21, 1986, I led my group and a squad of New York City Emergency Service officers on a raid of a house on Little Neck Parkway, Queens, New York. We surprised a fugitive Colombian cocaine dealer named Ricardo Peralta. Our timing was a little off, though; Peralta had just begun putting together a cocaine lab, so we didn't find any cocaine. But we did seize $50,000 in cash, a couple of guns, a new Jaguar automobile, and enough chemicals and other materials to charge him with setting up an illegal laboratory —all thanks to some alert suburbanite whose name we'll never know.[1]

EXAMPLE OF RURAL CITIZENS ALREADY IN ACTION

Nearly six hundred utility workers in forty-one Pennsylvania counties were organized into an intelligence network of "drug awareness teams" trained to alert police to possible drug lab sites. The Pennsylvania State Police instructed line workers, meter readers, and other employees in detecting indications of clandestine laboratories (see indications above).

"Rural electric workers travel the back roads and are in a better position to see things that normally go unnoticed," said Joseph Dukick, spokesman for the Pennsylvania Rural Electric Association of Harrisburg. "We told our people not to investigate. If they see something suspicious, turn and run in the other direction and contact the police."[2]

---

[1] U.S. v. Ricardo Peralta, case # C1-86-0240.
[2] "Pennsylvania Workers to Look for Drug Labs" (reprint of an AP news release), The New York Times, 11/24/89.

SUBURBAN ANTIDRUGGIE STRATEGIES

The third prong in our assault on drug *demand* in suburban and rural America—after the *Visual Threat* and *Street Tactics*—are the long- and short-range behind-the-scenes strategies, aimed at getting every element of our society to dedicate its resources to deterring the *demand* for drugs.

Law Enforcement

The suburban and rural community organizations must maintain an ongoing close and cooperative relationship with local law enforcement authorities, not only to achieve the goals of the community, but to show them the efficacy of devoting more of their efforts toward deterring the drug buyer as opposed to the mouse-on-a-treadmill chase of the dealers. They should constantly be kept appraised of successful antidruggie tactics used by other police departments (e.g., some of the examples cited in this book). And they should be made to feel that they are an important and integral part of your organization's activities.

Suburban and Rural Courts

The same tactics discussed earlier in this book are recommended in suburban and rural courts. Most of the judges and prosecutors are either elected officials and/or members of the same community or town represented by your organization. A strong, well-organized, well-focused BAD organization should have little difficulty in convincing its judges and prosecutors to make the local justice system a strong deterrent to the drug buyer.

EXAMPLE OF A SUBURBAN GROUP IN ACTION

A citizens' antidruggie group in Rochester, New York, calling itself "Rochester Fights Back Antidrug Coalition," used the media in an attempt to get the local justice system to be more of a deterrent against the user. The group—a coalition of several suburban and rural community organizations that pooled resources to unite Monroe County in one antidruggie front—issued a "task force" report blaming the courts for not serving "as a deterrent to the *use* of illegal drugs." The report said that "the failure of the criminal justice system to prosecute users" has, in essence, "effectively legalized" the use of drugs. Gordon Black, the head of the task force, said the war on drugs cannot be won "unless we succeed in driving down the demand for drugs."[1]

This is not only a perfect example of a community influencing the justice system, but of its effective use of the media to do it.

Media

In suburbia and rural America the media should be approached and used as recommended earlier in this book. There is, however, an additional tactic already proving itself effective in some suburban and rural communities—the publishing of the names of arrested druggies.

Since few druggies are ever convicted in court, the publishing of the names of those *arrested* in suburban and rural communities—where one's local reputation can have powerful effect on both personal and professional life—can be a mighty deterrent to potential drug buyers. If they know that

[1] "Antidrug Task Force Wants to Shift Priorities to Demand Side," UPI news release 1707, 3/27/90.

getting caught in *your* community gets their names in the newspaper, they will feel a strong urge to go elsewhere to buy their goodies, or quit. And if you can't get your local or county newspaper to do it, your group can print its own newspaper.

A Seminole, Florida, man, for example, is publishing a newspaper he calls *The Informer,* listing every local arrest. The publisher, Ray Aden, feels that his newspaper will act as a deterrent for all sorts of crimes, including drug offenses. According to Aden, "The great majority of people violating our laws are not known to their neighbors, their bosses, and sometimes even their families." Even civil libertarians agree that what Aden is doing is perfectly legal.[1]

"This is going to be a deterrent," said Aden. And I agree with him.

Liaison with Other Citizens' Organizations

It is important for all BAD, or any citizens' organizations with a like philosophy, to work in cooperation with and mutually support one another in both ridding their respective communities of druggies, and in spreading the philosophy of the BAD movement, until there are few places in America where the presence of druggies will be tolerated.

The key to doing this is voter power. The more groups and organizations linked together across our country acting as one, the bigger the voice and the sooner this disastrous and wasteful war on drugs will be ended. The citizens' war on drug abusers is no place for provincialism, racism, or anything else that divides us as a people. We are all affected equally and have the same interests at heart.

[1] James Martinez, "Murders-Rape-Abuse-DUI's-Drugs-Shoplifting-More," AP news release, 9/3/90.

Voter Power

I recommend that the suburban and rural community follow the recommendations listed earlier in this book under the same heading. In general, voter power in suburbia and rural America carries a lot more weight than in the huge, heavily populated urban areas. Suburban and rural citizens' antidruggie organizations, by mustering the vote, can immediately get the attention and cooperation of local politicians and bureaucrats, in finally implementing a sensible war against drug abusers and, with the successes that I am sure will result, start a grass roots movement that will be the herald of the end of this futile, sham war on drugs.

PART II

Druggie–Proofing the School

An education that does not cultivate the will is an education that depraves the mind.

—ANATOLE FRANCE,
The Crime of Sylvestre Bonnard (1881)

We're mad as hell and we just won't take it anymore. . . .

Amid reports indicating that as many as twenty-five percent of kids used drugs in school "most of the time," a group of parents in a small Ohio town decided they weren't going to tolerate it. They went to the school and volunteered to police the place themselves. It took a lot of parents and a lot of time, but they did it. The school was drug free.[1]

All it took was delivering a clear message: Druggies will not be tolerated here!

[1] Beth Polson and Miller Newton, Ph.D., *Not My Kid* (New York: Avon Books, 1985).

5

School Antidruggie Tactics

CONFUSED IMAGES

I spent a good portion of my career as a narcotics agent speaking at schools—from grade school to university level —on behalf of DEA, lecturing on "the evils of drugs." With my brother addicted to heroin and two growing children of my own, it was a labor of love. Also, being an expert in undercover tactics—which requires an understanding of human behavior that is second to none—I was insatiably curious as to *why* and *how* kids got started in drugs, the role schools might play, and what might be done to turn kids in other directions, *before* they began experimenting.

In 1975 I was invited to address my son Keith's fifth-grade class. The school, located in a northern suburb of New York City, was part of what was considered one of the best school systems in the country. They made quite a deal out of my speech, stopping class for the whole fifth grade and marching the kids down to the auditorium.

I'll never forget my son's face beaming with pride. The

program coordinator had told me that they were going to try and get permission for my daughter, then in the first grade, to leave class for a while to see some of her daddy's performance; but as it turned out they were unsuccessful until the last few embarrassingly tense moments of my presentation, when a teacher led her to the front of the packed auditorium to sit cross-legged on the floor; her face, below me, a tiny patch of pink, grinning pride. She had just missed the source of all the tension.

I had been asked to bring a film on drugs with me. Innocently, I called the DEA Public Affairs Section in Washington and asked for a film on drugs to show to "school kids." The day before my scheduled speech I received a wide, flat 16-millimeter film can containing a film called *The Perfect Pill.*

As I wound up my presentation on the evils of drugs and the derring-do of undercover agents, the visual aids technician was putting the finishing touches to the loading of the film onto the projector. When everything was set and they were about to turn the lights down, I winked at my son. He turned a proud crimson.

The film was about a high-school boy suffering all the typical problems and dilemmas of teenage years—girls, acne, identity, popularity, and so on—who decided that the solution to his seemingly endless anguish was finding a drug that would make him feel good all the time: the perfect pill.

The film started out innocently enough, looking as though it was going to be the typical pabulum served up by the drug education experts, featuring rock and roll music, wild teenage parties—something like the current crop of antidrug "rap" videos, that always leave me wondering whether they are really trying to promote drugs—followed by the obligatory overdose death scene and advice by some football star, movie star, or paid announcer to "say no to drugs," or something like that. I could not have been more wrong.

The bright, colorful images and upbeat music of teenage life soon changed to dark and somber depictions of druggie life and graphic scenes of what abuse actually does to the human body. One scene featured an overdosed teenager shuddering and jerking in grotesque, frothing convulsions. It was so realistic that I couldn't tell whether it was actual footage from an emergency room or great acting. The kids gasped and cringed around me. Some hid their eyes. One teacher was glaring at me so angrily that I could see the whites of her eyes glittering in the darkness.

When the lights came on I was faced with a silent sea of small faces and big, round frightened eyes, dotted here and there with the angry glares of teachers and parents. My poor little son looked like a lost puppy. After my daughter's arrival and a short question-and-answer session, the assembly was called to order and the kids marched silently out of the auditorium. The coordinator gave me a stiff handshake and thanked me politely for coming.

By the time I got back to my office in New York, the public affairs office had already received several complaint calls. Evidently I had used a film intended for an older audience and frightened the pants off the kids. The feeling among the teachers and parents present was that I had been insensitive in showing such a "graphic" film to so young an audience, and that I might have "seriously traumatized" some of them. No one in DEA took the incident seriously and it was soon forgotten. Needless to say, I was never invited back to speak at my children's school.

It wasn't until years later, when I was applying to DEA for a "hardship" transfer back to New York to rejoin my family and help my then thirteen-year-old daughter with her own drug-abuse problem that I remembered the incident. I was trying to understand why my son, who was then seventeen, had never even experimented with drugs and my daughter was about to destroy her life. I found myself wishing that my daughter had seen that film. My son, now a New York City police officer, had often told me of how that one film had had a very deep effect on him and many of his classmates.

It occurred to me that there was a definite parallel between my son's experience and one drawn from my own life. I was four years older than my brother David. He had started on heroin at fifteen years of age, and eventually committed suicide because of it. We had grown up together, yet I had never touched drugs. In searching my childhood for a reason, the only thing I kept coming up with was this feeling of mortal terror I had about drugs that seemed to stem from one incident.

When I was about thirteen I had seen the police removing an overdose victim from the hallway of a building, still a fairly rare sight in those years, even in the South Bronx. I can remember being unable to resist pushing through the crowd to get a closer look, and then being immediately sorry that I had. The cadaver was supposed to have been that of a teenaged boy, but the horribly grimacing face, with dead, fishlike eyes set above a mass of whitish nasal excretions, had no age. The hands, frozen in rigor mortis, seemed like two grotesque claws trying to fight their way back into life. The sight affected me deeply. It was an image that stayed with me for years and gave me many sleepless nights, yet I was thankful for it. I am convinced, at least in my case, that that one experience had been a strong psychological deterrent to my experimenting with drugs as a child.

Several months ago, after the publication of my book *Deep Cover*, I was invited to do a television show in San Diego, with parents and druggies in a local rehabilitation program. As it turned out, most of the "rehabilitating" addicts had "relapsed" numerous times and had been through a multiplicity of treatment and rehabilitation programs. "Relapse is part of the rehabilitation process," explained the head of the program—a story that every head of every rehab program in America will tell you.

Well, what else can they tell you? It's either that, or the truth: they don't know how to stop people from taking drugs.

I told the studio audience and the camera that I believed that parading rehabilitated, or rehabilitating, drug addicts in front of schools and on television was a poor example for kids. My reasoning was: Why should that kind of moral weakness be rewarded with all that attention? I thought we should make an effort to find those few kids who had resisted peer pressure and *never* tried drugs and make *them* the heroes; reward *them* with all the attention; make *them* the object lesson in front of the classroom. It was *their* advice kids should seek, and not that of some yo-yo who, in spite of the hundreds of millions we spend on "antidrug" education, became a druggie anyway; or some professional athlete who got a "league suspension" for his second or third drug offense and was doing "community service."

God protect us from them. That kind of stupidity should not be rewarded in any way. If you manage to get yourself drug free in a rehabilitation program, great. Congratulations! You did yourself and your poor, suffering family a service. But we won't put you in front of young children in schools whom we want to dissuade from using or experimenting with drugs for the first time. You are *not* an example for anyone to follow.

Of course, the rehab people were up in arms. "The gangs and ghetto kids can't relate to those kinds of kids," said one expert. A teenaged Mexican-American girl in the studio audience raised her hand to speak. She said that she had grown up in the gangs yet had never even experimented with drugs and did not see the need for rehabilitated druggies to "relate to" or as advisors. "I didn't need anyone to tell me what drugs did," she said. "I saw it right in front of me, and I didn't want it to happen to me."

As the girl spoke I flashed back to my own youth. I knew exactly what she meant. I could feel the truth in her words. The ugliness of what drug abuse does to the human body and mind speaks eloquently for itself in horrific real-life images. Images that can be particularly effective weapons in shaping children's attitudes toward experimenting with drugs—if they are exposed to them, graphically, at an early enough age.

Even more important is the changing of children's attitudes toward the drug user. One of the main reasons for the failure of our massive federal antidrug educational program is *its* failure to address itself to the main cause of the spread of drugs in our schools—the drug user. As Dr. Ian Macdonald, former drug expert in the Reagan White House, pointed out, the spread of drug abuse "occurs, almost without exception, between an established drug user and a novice, within a very close friendship."[1] It's a pity that Dr. Macdonald's viewpoint was never translated into action by our government.

My own two decades of questioning druggies indicated that Dr. Macdonald could not have been more accurate. Almost every single one I have come in contact with began using drugs given him or her by a "friend," a schoolmate, at a party or some other social gathering. And a high proportion of these had their initial drug experiences, directly or indirectly, through a school contact.

[1] Dr. Carl T. Rowan, "Let's Get Tough With Drug Users," *Reader's Digest,* July 1989.

In spite of this knowledge we are still failing to warn our children that their buddy, schoolmate, playmate, or friend who uses drugs is the real enemy—the one they have most to fear. Even the phrase "Say no to drugs"—the title of our federal government's educational program—is as confused and misleading as the program itself. It implies that *drugs* are the enemy, and further confuses our children into the belief that they are not responsible for their choice.

The politicians, bureaucrats, and experts adhering to the Big Lie, insisting that drug abuse is caused by foreign drug dealers and "the availability of drugs on our streets"; or those who categorize the drug problem as a plague, epidemic, or—as Senator Joseph Biden did—as "a public health emergency," further confuse our children into believing the drug problem is viral, biochemical, or the end result of "a war" being waged against us; and that the people "hit" by the drug problem are poor unfortunates who should bear none of the moral responsibility of their actions.

And where society in general, and our schools in particular, have failed most in arming our children to protect themselves from drug abuse is in the portrayal of the druggie. Instead of the schools' teaching a healthy disdain for druggies—in kids' parlance making it "uncool" to take drugs—we have been doing the opposite.

Our children are daily treated to the highly publicized arrests of druggies from the top of the worlds of sports, show business, and politics—"stars" whom they had been taught to emulate. Then they see these same stars "rehabilitated" and greeted as returning heroes, coming to their schools, either as part of a court sentence of "community service" or appearing on television, telling them, "Don't do as I did. Drugs are bad for you." They see movies and television shows that glamorize drugs and graphic violence, and advertising that sells every form of escape from reality that the imagination can conjure.

Yet films like the one I showed my son's fifth-grade class are considered "too graphic" for young children.

Then they hear politicians, judges, experts and, sadly, educators arguing for the legalization of drugs. And, as is happening too often, they are witness to the drug abuse of their own parents. And then we wonder why our children are turning to drugs as never before and why our schools—instead of being a force to turn the tide—have become "hotbeds" and "breeding grounds" for druggies.

Cutting through the Hypocrisy

Unfortunately, our experts and leaders still have us fighting the same fraudulent, failed war "against drugs" in our schools. Once again it is going to be left to us, as citizens, to do what government has been unable to do. The community that has organized itself against the drug abuser—not against drugs, the dealers, the evil drug barons, or the KGB —can quickly and effectively insure that its schools are free of drug problems, and at the same time combat the hypocrisy and ambiguities of our so-called war on drugs with a clear-cut and unequivocal message for its children:

> It's not "cool" to be a druggie; druggies exemplify the worst of human behavior, and will be tolerated neither on our streets nor in our schools.

It is a message that should be reinforced by giving the children an alternative "tough," "cool," nondruggie image that even the most rebellious child would want to emulate.

THE BAD ORGANIZATION'S ROLE AND GOALS IN THE SCHOOL

Once we have accepted the fact that the key to stopping the spread of drug abuse in the school, as well as on the street, is the isolation and control of the druggie, our course is clear. We want to make our community's schools as inhospitable for druggies as our streets. The strong antidruggie message and feelings exemplified by the community's visible and tactical actions on the streets and elsewhere should already have gone a long way to inspire a very healthy disdain and intolerance for druggies on the part of its children. It is a sentiment that not only should wash over into the schools—it must be fortified there.

To be certain that this happens the community organization should have three main goals: first, to take all possible physical security measures to insure that the presence of a single drug abuser in school is not tolerated and that the school environment is as hostile toward drug abusers as the neighborhood; second, to seek the implementation of an anti–drug-abuse education program that would present the image of the druggie as the anathema to society that he is and instill in the students a "fearful" respect for the physical and mental damages caused by substance abuse; third, to create an alternative, nondruggie image the children would want to emulate.

To achieve these goals the community organization must adopt an active role in its schools. One of the biggest mistakes a community organization can make is to *leave it to the experts*. Remember: In the drug war there are no experts; but there are plenty of villains. Druggie schoolteachers, and even principals, are being arrested with increasing frequency. And most communities around the country— while organizing to fight drugs on the streets—pay little or no attention to the kind of drug education their children are receiving in school. They've left that for the experts, which can lead to some unwanted surprises. A case in point: The parents of one New York City school district—District 10, the largest local district in the city, responsible for the education of some 37,000 students—were shocked to learn that the district itself had published a booklet for its kids that downplayed the dangers of marijuana and advised the children to hide drugs from police and paramedics in the event a friend overdoses.[1]

Incredible, but true!

It is therefore imperative for a community organized against drug abusers to carry its fight into the schools, and leave nothing to the experts. This means that group representatives should endeavor to be actively interested and involved in *all* activities of its community schools.

ANTIDRUGGIE SECURITY MEASURES

1. *The interviewing, screening, and hiring of teachers*

The main concern here is that the prospective teacher— or any other professional or paraprofessional coming in daily contact with the students—not have any indication of drug abuse in his or her past. A community organization should insist on a criminal-record check and drug testing, before the hiring, or even the interviewing, of any prospective teacher. We test police, firemen, and others in occupations responsible for public safety; are we going to risk our children's health in untested hands? What is most important is that the children are aware of the community's con-

---

[1] Rob Polner, "Schoolbook Says 'Hide Drugs,' " *New York Post,* 1/16/90. According to the article, a representative in the school district said the booklet is no longer being bought.

cern and active vigilance in keeping *all* druggies out of the schools—be they students or teachers.

2. *The creation of a tough drug-offender policy*

The most important stated goal of a school's anti–drug-abuse policy—more important than the usual prohibitions against sale, use, and possession of drugs and paraphernalia —is the absolute refusal to tolerate the presence of *any* drug abusers in the school system. This must be stated in clear, unequivocal terms. Some officials in neighborhood schools with extremely high drug-abuse problems will throw up their hands and ask, "What do I do, expel half the school?" The answer is: Yes, if necessary.

When the now famous Joe Clark (portrayed by actor Morgan Freeman in the movie *Lean on Me*) became principal of Eastside High School in Paterson, New Jersey, he inherited a school that was rampant with druggies who in turn attracted dealers and armed gangs right into the hallways and bathrooms of the school. The school was a wide-open drug bazaar; an extension of the tough inner-city streets just outside. In Mr. Clark's first year on the job he warned all druggies that if they were caught, they were out. He then backed up his warning by expelling three hundred students for drug violations. His first concern was protecting the students who had come to learn. Within one year Eastside High School rose from zoolike anarchy to become a smoothly functioning place of learning.[1]

a. *Penalties (in general).* The penalties for drug violations should take two factors into consideration. The first, and most important, is the protection of the children who come to school to learn. If it is found that the offender has—as most druggies do—enticed others to use drugs, I

[1] *Schools Without Drugs,* published by U.S. Department of Education, 1987, page 22.

would recommend his or her *arrest and expulsion.* Whether the drugs were sold or given away does not matter. Drugs received as "gifts" from "friends" account for the vast majority of first-time experiences; thus, *giving the drugs away* can be looked upon as a lot more serious an act than sale.[2] The existence of this type of regulation will demonstrate to the children the gravity of that kind of behavior, and that it will *never* be tolerated. There should be no exceptions to this rule.

The second consideration is for the possible rehabilitation of the offender caught with drugs or paraphernalia for his or her own use. (My own daughter was in this category. I'll discuss her case later in this book.) Since the usual course of drug addiction is occasional use, to regular use, to addiction and multiple drug use, an effort should be made to determine the stage of the addictive process of the offender. The earlier caught, the better chance for rehabilitation.

Here is where a specialist from one of the behavioral sciences might be consulted, depending on each school's situation and on the parent's wishes. A school with a rampant drug problem, as was the case with principal Joe Clark's school, may not have the time or resources to become involved with treatment and rehabilitation, and must remain focused on protecting the rights of those children who are *not* drug users.

What is most important is that the school draw a very clear and definite limit beyond which it will not tolerate any recidivism. The sterner the limit the more inspiration the druggie has to straighten himself out, and the clearer

[2] Carl T. Rowan, "Let's Get Tough With Drug Users," *Reader's Digest,* July 1989.

the message delivered to the rest of the children: Druggies will not be tolerated here!

Principal Joe Clark's stern measures succeeded in turning around the lives of a hell of a lot of kids who were on the edge of the abyss; and saved the lives of a lot of druggies who, finding themselves confronted with a system they could not beat, cleaned themselves up and joined it instead.

b. *Codification of offenses and penalties.* The written version of the school's code of conduct, as it pertains to drugs, should be carefully prepared and worded with the collaboration and advice of local prosecuting attorneys, law-enforcement officers, and the school's legal counsel. The BAD organization should take part in its writing and/or its amendment, to insure that it is the expression of the *community's* attitude toward drug abusers; and that the very wording of the code be a stern warning to them.

I like the pejorative use of the term *druggie.* The word, in itself, is a expression of the community's disgust with the people it describes. I don't think we should lose any opportunity in expressing that disgust to our children, and would recommend it being written into the Code of Conduct, to describe those who violate it. The following areas should be covered:

(1). What constitutes an offense (possession, sale, use, possession of paraphernalia, et cetera, including definitions of each "substance" forbidden on school property).

(2). What area or jurisdiction should be considered "school property" or under "school jurisdiction."

(3). Who, specifically, has the authority to detain or arrest a student, including specific procedures in the handling of the violator (when parents, police, or legal counsel are called, and so on).

(4). Due process; the method by which each violation will be ultimately resolved (a hearing before the principal, the school board, et cetera).

(5). Penalties for infractions.

SIGNED BY PARENTS AND STUDENTS

A final version of the school's drug code, with a clear, unmistakable warning that violators are subject to ARREST and EXPULSION, *must* be read and signed by every student and his or her parents.

WARNING SIGNS POSTED

Signs, warning that the school prohibits *all* druggie activity, and that such activity will end in arrest and expulsion, should be visibly posted around the school.

3. *The creation of an environment hostile to drug abuse*

a. *Creation of a school anti–drug-abuse office.* An office should be created within the school, combining school, community, and *most importantly* student representatives, whose sole purposes are the prevention of drug abuse and the identification, segregation, and removal of drug abusers from the school. This should be the headquarters, the record keeping, coordination, and liaison center for the school anti–drug-abuse efforts. It is important that all efforts be centrally run and monitored, and that the office not deviate from its very specialized mission.

b. *Physical security.* The community organization, working in cooperation with the neighborhood school board, police, and prosecutor's office, should organize whatever physical presence, in the form of hallway and grounds patrols, security checkpoints, visitor log books, deemed necessary. The *primary* purpose of this presence must be to identify and remove drug abusers from the school; the *secondary* purpose—prevention—is to create an environment hostile to drug abuse.

Once again, the focus of all activities is against drug abusers—not drugs in general, nor dealers, who should be considered a police problem. This accomplishes three very important goals: First, you are ridding the school of the primary cause of the spread of drug use; second, you are ridding the school of a drug customer (one less reason for a dealer to exist), and finally, you are hammering away at the message of how completely unacceptable that kind of behavior is and how *uncool* and demeaning it is to be a lowly, unwanted druggie.

Remember, by catching the druggie as early as you can in his romance with disaster, you will be doing him and his family a favor that may lead to his rescue.

This, of course, does not mean that drug dealers are to be ignored. They should be handled in the same way the neighborhood patrol handles them—get all the evidence you can as instructed by the police, and turn it over to the police. If you are coordinating your efforts with the police (as you should be), don't worry about it; they will instruct you. And if you are effectively combating the druggie and his image, you soon won't have a dealer problem.

c. *Creation of a student antidruggie security patrol.* Student participation in school antidruggie security and patrol activities is a great opportunity to give even the most rebellious students an image to emulate. The Guardian Angels are martial-arts-trained young men and women who, armed with nothing more than their distinctive red berets and T-shirts and working as unpaid volunteers, have managed to cut crime—particularly drug-related crime—in almost every area they have ever patrolled. And they have fearlessly entered some of the toughest inner-city neighborhoods in our nation. There is nothing wimpy about their image, and they *don't* do drugs.

I recommend forming a Guardian Angels type of patrol unit in the school as a vital part of the community's antidruggie measures; and that as much of the security patrol work as is practically possible be made the exclusive responsibility of students.

d. *Physical signs that drugs are being used in school.* The finding of physical signs that drugs are being used in the school will quickly tip you off to what locations have to be more closely observed by security patrols.

(1). Drug paraphernalia (rolling paper, crack vials, and so on) in the hallways, bathrooms, and grounds of the school.

(2). The odor of drugs and incense.

(3). The secretive congregating of students in a particular location.

e. *Signs indicating a student who may be a drug abuser.* The school is *the* most difficult place for a druggie to remain invisible; his erratic behavior is unmistakable. Any combination of the following observations, easily made in the school setting, are good indications that you are dealing with a druggie (for a more detailed list of "signs of drug abuse," see Part III, Family Self-Defense):

(1). General appearance. Druggies tend to let their appearance go as their dependence grows, paying less and less attention to their hygiene and grooming. Their clothing will tend to be disheveled, their eyes bloodshot with dilated pupils and, in general—except for beginning users—will have a decidedly unhealthy look about them.

(2). The wearing of drug-oriented insignias on clothing, drug paraphernalia and jewelry (gold and silver coke spoons and marijuana leaf pendants, et cetera), and the possession of drug-culture magazines.

(3). Changes in classroom performance. Suddenly falling grades, uncompleted assignments, difficulty in concentration, slurred speech, a lack of motivation energy and concern for grades, short attention span and memory lapses, a lack of interests and outside hobbies.

(4). Poor attendance.

(5). Changes in personality. An inability to get along well with others; incidents of inappropriate anger, hostility, paranoia, and secretiveness.

(6). Chronic lying, stealing, cheating.

(7). Trouble with the police.

(8). Possession of inordinate amounts of cash.

f. *Warning, identifying, and isolating the druggies.* The school should issue a general warning that very stern measures are about to be taken against everyone determined to be a druggie; that he is going to be offered an opportunity to turn himself in for treatment without fear of any disciplinary action; and that all those later identified as drug abusers, who do not turn themselves in for treatment, will be immediately suspended and (should the situation warrant it) expelled.

If this sounds familiar, it is because the idea is modeled somewhat loosely after what Japan and China did. If their experience is any indication of what can be expected —once the community has already taken action on its streets, and its warning in the schools is perceived as one with real "teeth"—then many students will turn themselves in. Your group will not only be drastically curtailing the spread of drug abuse to nonusers, but will be saving the lives of some of the druggies as well.

The parents of all those students suspected of being drug abusers should be contacted immediately and informed of the reasons behind your suspicions, along with their options.

g. *Anti–drug-abuser activities and tactics.*

(1). *Observing student behavior.* Community citizens' patrols, student patrols, teachers, and school staff, working in close coordination with parents, should be on the alert for all signs of drug abuse. Suspected violators should be identified and observed closely.

(2). *Patrols and surveillance on school grounds.* The community organization, working in close cooperation with parents, the school staff, and local police, should institute hallway and grounds patrols, a visitor and hallway pass system, and the possible installation of video surveillance cameras in hallways and stairwells and areas suspected of being used for drug taking. *As many of these activities as possible should be made the responsibility of the students themselves.* The precise systems and tactics employed should be worked out with the advice of attorneys and narcotics enforcement experts, and should be tailored to the gravity of the problem.

(3). *Surveillance of the neighborhood surrounding the school.* School-age drug abusers are, more often than not, going to do their thing away from school property —especially once strong antidruggie measures have been instituted on the school grounds. During school hours the neighborhood BAD patrol, working closely with police, will want to observe areas around the school very closely.

(4).*Utilizing local police in reverse undercover operations.* In severe situations the community and school might want to request that local law-enforcement authorities institute periodic reverse undercover operations. Recently, the state of New Jersey demonstrated how effective this type of enforcement can be in the school. State police undercover agents posing as drug dealers hung around schools and sold heavily diluted cocaine to unsuspecting young druggie buyers and then arrested them. A state prosecutor said that the program had great promise as a deterrent because of a survey that indicated that "the thing that young people fear the most is getting into trouble for using drugs."[1]

h. *Search and arrest powers and the law.* Members of the community organization, student patrols, teachers, and school staff should learn the limits of the law in detaining and searching students suspected of violation of the drug laws. These activities should be closely coordinated with the local prosecutor's office and police as to the specifics of policy and action.

The laws governing the privacy rights of students is ever changing. In 1985 the Supreme Court sought to define a law that would balance the rights of students against unreasonable searches and seizures versus the need for schools to maintain order. In general, the Supreme Court has, along with decisions of lower courts, given schools the following rights:

(1). School officials may institute a search if there are "reasonable grounds" to believe that the search will reveal that the student is violating either the law or school rules.

(2). School officials may search *without a warrant* as long as they are conducting a search on school property, and *no law-enforcement authorities* are involved in

---

[1] Reginald Roberts, "Troopers Make Drug Buyers Beware in Passaic," *Newark Star Ledger*, 6/24/89.

the search. This includes students' personal lockers. Some courts have held that schools may institute a policy authorizing school officials to inspect school lockers at any time, without the necessity of showing "reasonable grounds."

(3). School officials may conduct a search that is as extensive as necessary (e.g., body-cavity search), considering the circumstances surrounding the search, the age and sex of the student being searched, and the nature of the evidence or contraband being sought. In general, the more intrusive the search, the greater the justification necessary.

i. *Arrest, suspension, and expulsion.* Once drug abusers have been identified, caught, arrested, or confronted, the school's policies must be rigidly adhered to with no exceptions. The perception that there is no way of "beating the system" is of utmost importance in dealing with druggies.

It is equally important that the rest of the students understand that the stern, no-nonsense treatment of drug abusers is an expression of the community's disgust and intolerance for them; that druggies are not "victims"; and that the purpose of these regulations is to protect students who don't want to associate with or be pressured by them.

If a druggie has been caught in the act, or proven beyond a reasonable doubt to have sold or given away drugs to others, I once again recommend his or her arrest and immediate suspension, followed by—if the facts and circumstances warrant it—expulsion. Once the matter is turned over to the police it will not be a problem for the school unless the druggie applies for readmittance (discussed below). The community organization must do all it can to insure that the school is inflexible in the enforcement of this rule. It will leave an important and indelible message inscribed on the student psyche: that there will be no bargaining with the type of reprehensible behavior typified by druggies.

For drug abusers, whom school policy indicates should be expelled or suspended, federal law requires that they be afforded the basic constitutional protection of "due process." That means they have the right to a formal hearing and adjudication of the charges against them. I would recommend that these hearings—as is the case with all criminal and civil trials and hearings—be open to the public, that they be held in the school auditorium or a place large enough to accommodate the entire student body, and that, to as great an extent as possible, they be made the responsibility of the students themselves.

j. *Initiate a student court system.* The Rockland County, New York, schools have initiated a "student court" system, wherein the students themselves are the judges, juries, and prosecuting and defense attorneys. I went through the system myself when my daughter was caught on school grounds with marijuana. The students have the power of suspending or recommending expulsion for *all* infractions of the school code, including drugs. They also have the power to sentence student "violators" to "community or school service." It is a system that I would highly recommend.

k. *Rehabilitation of expelled or suspended druggies. When is a druggie accepted as rehabilitated and allowed to return to school?*

By allowing the readmittance of an expelled drug abuser who has failed at rehabilitation *more* than once, you are undermining your whole program by creating a perception that you can "beat the system"—something the druggie character seems to take great joy in doing.

But most importantly, you are putting the rest of the children at risk. Never forget that it is characteristic of *all* druggies to want to seduce everyone and anyone around them into "doing" drugs with them. That is why they get the whole blame for the spread of drug abuse. And in a school setting the safety and education of non–drug-abusing children must come *before* concerns about the treatment and rehabilitation of druggies—concerns that are supposed to be dealt with by rehabilitation experts.

Thus, I would recommend a school policy that gives drug abusers one chance, and one chance only, to rehabilitate; and that readmittance to school *only* be permitted—subject to advice of counsel—if the drug abuser voluntarily undergoes regular and frequent testing from the time of readmittance. Taking this kind of positive, no-nonsense stand will be doing the druggie and his family a favor—possibly saving his or her life—and will be for the good of the rest of the students.

6

Antidruggie Education

Education, properly understood, is that which teaches discernment.
—Joseph Roux, *Meditations of a Parish Priest* (1886),
tr. Isabel F. Hapgood.

REALISTIC ANTI–DRUG-ABUSE EDUCATION PROGRAM

Drug experts spend most of their time and our money in frantic searches for statistics, any statistics whatsoever, that will justify their massive expenditures on antidrug education programs that do not work. Former Drug Czar William Bennett, for example, once cited a study that indicated that drug abuse, in general, was declining. For the ex-Czar —a onetime secretary of education and a man alleged to be an expert both on education and drugs—it was truly a statistic from heaven. He launched himself at the media with a new phrase. On an *Evans and Novak* show he said, "America is undergoing what I like to call 'the great American change of mind.' "[1]

A week later another study was picked up by the wire services, indicating there were actually twice the number of drug abusers than the first study had claimed. This brought

[1] *Evans and Novak,* broadcast on Cable News Network, 4/15/90.

the Czar back to the little tube, along with Senator Joseph Biden, in an argument over who had misinterpreted the statistics. The astonishing discussion, typical of the political game our war on drugs has evolved into, ended with Czar Bennett convincing Senator Biden that while the problem might not have improved, it had "leveled out."

The important point highlighted by this incident is that, while our antidrug education programs continue to be massive failures, those responsible for them—the Czars (now we have a new one, an out-of-work politician named Bob Martinez), the politicians, the suits, whoever—aren't seeking to study, change, and make educational programs more effective, they are instead in a mad scramble to justify themselves and the torrents of taxpayer dollars they are spending. It is not that this crop of suits and politicians are any better or worse than those who have come before them for the past three decades. It simply means that when it comes to the problem of drug abuse, we simply cannot rely on politicians and bureaucrats for *real* solutions—especially not in the schools.

Just how ineffective our current drug education program is was best illustrated in a *Wall Street Journal* article about the Bainbridge Island, Washington, school system.[1]

Why Bainbridge, Washington? Well, aside from the fact that the Bainbridge school system has a serious drug problem typical of most of the schools systems in our nation—five percent of the students chemically dependent and seventy percent using drugs and/or alcohol on a weekly basis—scholastically, Bainbridge is rated as one of the nation's top school systems, and for the last twelve years has been running "one of the most intensive and innovative antidrug

[1] Joseph Pereira, "Even a School That Is a Leader in Drug War Grades Itself a Failure," *The Wall Street Journal,* 11/10/90.

programs in the country." The program has been a resounding failure.

Incredibly, the Bush-Bennett drug education programs, *now* being introduced to schools across the country, are identical to the ones Bainbridge has had in place for twelve years.

According to the article Bainbridge's frustration is "echoed by educators around the country" who have complained that "too little research has been done into the effectiveness of the numerous types of drug education programs in use." Robert Ryan, an administrator with California's Department of Education, said, "We've thrown $45 million over the last three years into drug education in our schools. But as of yet I don't think we can say what helps and what doesn't."

How can our government continue to shovel billions of dollars into programs that are called ineffective by the very people running them? I don't know. But I do know that a community organization can, on its own, turn the situation around by insisting that its voice be heard in deciding what type of anti–drug-abuse training its children receive.

What kind of anti–drug-abuse education do we want our kids to have?

To answer this, let's examine the Bainbridge system—keeping in mind that it is the prototype of the drug-abuse educational programs being instituted across the nation—and understand why it fails. It seems to me that the main problem with the Bainbridge approach is that it is based on the assumption that the presentation of information about drugs to children, in a classroom setting, combined with role playing (practicing how to "say no to drugs"), classes on "self-esteem," and motivational speeches by experts, celebrities, and rehabilitated druggies, would in some mysterious way guide behavior away from experimenting with drugs.

It sounds nice, but it just doesn't work.

"It would give me great pride to say that we've done [the antidrug education system] for twelve years and it's really working," said Julia Wan, Bainbridge's assistant superintendent of schools, "but it's not the case."

Success in the manipulation and control of behavior, whether of adults or children, as any undercover agent or Madison Avenue advertising executive knows, is largely a matter of presentation. If you want to create a hunger for something, you present it in a way that makes the mouth water. If you want to create an aversion, you portray it in a way that will inspire loathing, suspicion, fear, and disgust, or any combination thereof. And to prevent our children from experimenting with drugs, the aversions we want to create are against two things: drug abusers and drugs. Specifically, our goals with respect to each should be:

• *Drug Abusers.* We want to create a suspicion and healthy loathing for druggies and all that druggie behavior typifies.

• *Drugs.* We want to create a *fearful* respect for the damage that illegal drugs and the abuse of legal drugs can do.

1. *The druggie's image*

The Bainbridge school system—as did most school systems in our nation—instituted what they called an *"Antidrug* Education Program." The title alone has kids on the wrong track right from the start. Our nation's school systems are learning the hard way that a child's druggie friend can overcome twelve years of Say-no-to-drugs training with a simple: "Are you too chicken to try it?"

The experts call it "peer pressure"; a phrase that is not specific enough. Fighting the abstract, *peer pressure,* is as useless as our war against the inanimate, *drugs.* It is not *just* peer pressure that causes our kids to try drugs; it is pressure from a particular type of peer—the druggie. To defeat "druggie pressure," parents and educators must attack the image of the druggie in such a way that he is the last thing in the world a child would want to emulate.

I can't think of anything more damaging to a program aimed at combating druggie pressure than putting a rehabilitated druggie onstage, on television, or at the head of a classroom, as someone whose advice children should follow —a position, to most of us, occupied by people we admire. Dick Hayes, the head of the U.S. Education Department's drug-prevention program, put it succinctly when he said, "One of the dangers of using recovered addicts in prevention programs is that we might be giving a mixed message— 'I tried it. I've recovered and I'm driving away in my BMW.' "[1] He is one of the very few education experts I've heard say anything similar. The problem is that no one is paying any attention to him.

I believe—and I think the massive failure of our national education and prevention programs bear me out—that it is like a commercial *for* drug abuse. It sends a message that an easy way to get attention, to become a person people respect and admire—like the druggie onstage—is to take drugs.

I cringe every time I see some so-called rehabilitated druggie—who, according to all statistics available, will soon relapse back into drug abuse—sharply dressed, speaking with poise and self-confidence (they all learn the Don't-do-as-I-did rap by heart) to an audience of nonuser children, or

[1] Linda Ellerbee, "Education Dept.'s Drug Drive Fails," *New York Post,* 7/19/90.

children who are still at the experimenting stage, presenting a glamorous sort of rebel image; the kind of guy or girl a kid would want as his buddy or confidant—someone to emulate. It may be great therapy for the druggie, but it is absolute devastation to our children.

And when the ex-druggie is a celebrity, you can multiply the damage tenfold. Judges who sentence famous druggies to do penance by making antidrug speeches in the media and in schools are doing more damage to our kids than the Medellín cartel and Colonel Noriega combined.

If the treatment experts believe they have a successfully rehabilitated druggie and want him used as an example to follow, they ought to put him before an audience of druggies undergoing treatment, much in the same way Alcoholics Anonymous uses recovering alcoholics—*never* before an audience of nonuser children.

If you want to show children how *bad* it is to abuse drugs and how thoroughly repulsive and degrading it is to be a drug abuser, you don't present druggies at their best. Instead of inviting them to speak at your school, organize field trips and observe them slumped over and whining in jail cells with open toilets stinking from excrement; or convulsing and vomiting on themselves in detoxification wards; or staring vacant eyed on the benches of intake centers and emergency wards. *That is what being a druggie is really all about, and that is what we should want our kids to see and understand.*

Schools Without Drugs—the U.S. Government book of advice on how to keep your schools drug free—begins with a quote from a Washington, D.C., seventh-grader: "We have a right to be protected from drugs."[1] If she had been edu-

---

[1] *Schools Without Drugs*, published by U.S. Department of Education, 1987, page IV, comment made by Cicely Senior, a seventh-grader at MacFarland Junior High, Washington, D.C.

cated in a BAD neighborhood school she would have said, "We have a right to be protected from these disgusting, low-life druggies. Please get them out of our schools and off our backs, so that we can learn."

A BAD community's school's antidruggie education program should have as its number-one priority that the druggie be portrayed accurately. Representatives of the organization, designated to work within the school system, should do everything in their power to see that, as part of its community school's drug abuse, education, and prevention programs:

a. Children are taught to be wary of classmates and friends who use drugs as the most likely source of their first experimental drug and that the act of offering drugs to someone to "get high" is one of the most despicable acts one human can commit against another; and that the druggie is *not* a victim, but a fool.

b. Children are presented with accurate portrayals—via video, film, live theater, or field trips to jails, drug intake centers, emergency rooms, detoxification centers, and police holding tanks—of the true-to-life loathsome image and behavior of *real* druggies.

c. The cruelty and inhuman acts that druggies commit so casually should also be *shown* to students. Some suggestions might be: a field trip to a crack-baby ward where the sight of rows of tiny, convulsing little babies fighting desperately for life would speak eloquently of the inhumanity of druggie mothers; or inviting the mothers, fathers, and grandparents who have been beaten and robbed by their own druggie children and grandchildren to speak to students—instead of recovering druggies.

d. Rehabilitated or rehabilitating druggies are *never* permitted to counsel or otherwise advise nonuser children as a method of drug-abuse prevention.

e. Awards and scholarship programs are instituted for leadership and individuality, and for those students who have most exhibited strength of character by overcoming life's difficulties and hardships *without* turning to drugs.

f. Student activities in school antidrug and -crime patrols, student courts, and other community service must be emphasized as much as sports and scholastic activities and rewarded with scholarships and other awards.

2. *A realistic drug education*

What is dangerous about the tranquilizers is that whatever peace of mind they bring is a packaged peace of mind. Where you buy a pill and buy peace with it, you get conditioned to cheap solutions instead of deep ones.
—Max Lerner, "The Assault on the Mind," *The Unfinished Country* (1959)

The notion of going to war against "drugs" has another downside that few people seem to consider. Most of our educational programs teach children, as early as in the first or second grades, to "say no to drugs," when often in their lives it may be prescribed "drugs" that they will need to restore their health and mental balance and save their lives. Children, already the victim of so many of our society's double messages, have to be given the straight scoop if you want them to respond. For an anti–drug-abuse education to be effective the community organization should influence its schools to:

a. Institute mandatory courses and lectures on the damage that substance abuse does to the human body and brain, featuring *realistic* and *graphic* examples of that damage.

b. Organize field trips to hospitals, emergency wards, and—particularly for students suspected of being in the early stages of drug abuse—morgues.

c. Invite the local medical examiner to the school for a presentation about drug-related deaths. Most MEs have a collection of slides and photos of overdose deaths for these occasions. I remember seeing a show put on at DEA's New York headquarters by Michael Bader, the New York City medical examiner, that even affected a few street-hardened narcotics agents.

The frightening truth about the havoc drug abuse wreaks on the human body, live and in vivid color, will not affect all the kids, but for those it does, the effort is well worth it.

Any drug abuse message to kids has to be free of hypocrisy and have a ring of truth to it, or they will just plain laugh at it, ignore it, or worse: rebel against it.

A Bainbridge high school student described an all-night drug and alcohol binge as "the ultimate defiance of everything we learned about the evil of drugs." He said that they were so stoned by morning that they didn't know who would remain conscious. Still each continued drinking and taking drugs and with each swig or snort announced, "See you in the emergency room," in disdainful reference to school antidrug advisories they'd seen in class. Today the student is a recovering addict and his friends still get stoned on weekends.

It merits repeating that the Bainbridge antidrug education program is the prototype of all the programs our government is now beginning to institute around the country.[1]

[1] Joseph Pereira, "Even a School That Is a Leader in Drug War Grades Itself a Failure," *The Wall Street Journal,* 11/10/90.

The article reminded me of the incident at my son's school. The graphic film I had accidentally shown was nothing to scorn or laugh at; it was the *real* thing. The reaction of the children was a stunned silence. And they had been exposed to it at a very impressionable age. Many of them probably forgot the images they had seen—but there were a few, like my son, who did not. The film didn't *say* drugs were evil and bad for you, it *showed* exactly what drugs did. The kids, teachers, and parents were shocked; yet by today's standards I would say the film was too mild.

Unfortunately, no matter what lengths a community goes to in making its schools safe, drug-free centers of learning, there will always be a few children who will fall. Experts will ramble on and on about the same socioeconomic, racial, genetic, cultural, and deep-rooted psychological causes for substance abuse they've been rambling on about for decades, without curing a single druggie. Let them. They probably mean well. In the meantime your community will have achieved the druggie-free learning environment your children need and deserve.

Project DARE

Before the publication of this book I checked with some of my colleagues in the American Federation of Former Narcotics Agents (AFFNA)—an organization dedicated to finding real solutions to our nation's drug problems—for ideas and input. Many of the members—among them the current heads of various police departments around the country—were so enthusiastic about project DARE (Drug-Abuse Resistance Education), that I decided to include it in the text.

The project, begun by the Los Angeles Police Department in cooperation with its city school system, began in

1983 and has since spread to cities and towns as far flung as Las Vegas, Nevada, Paramus, New Jersey, and Boston, Massachusetts. It is an eighteen-week program, using police officers as teachers, aimed at building self-esteem in elementary-level schoolchildren in order to arm them with the "strength" to reject peer pressure and say an emphatic *no* to drugs.

From the enthusiastic support and votes of confidence the project is getting from law enforcement, educators, and parents in the areas where it has already been instituted, I would highly recommend that it be considered, *in addition* to the above recommendations, in your school system.

PART III

Family Self-Defense

Selfishness is not living as one wishes to live, it is asking others to live as one wishes to live.

—OSCAR WILDE,
The Soul of Man Under Socialism (1891)

7
Prevention

If you are lucky enough to live in a community with a BAD-type organization, the community's strong antidruggie attitudes will go a long way in instilling an attitude of fear and revulsion toward drug abuse in general and druggies in particular; and in itself will be a strong preventative measure affecting all the community's children. Whether or not you live in such a neighborhood, the best time to stop a drug problem is long before it begins.

In spite of my misgivings about so-called expert advice in solving our drug problems, I tried to read with an open mind everything available on what they had to say about prevention. Sadly, what I found is that the American parent is in dire need of realistic advice; if you've read one expert's opinion you've pretty much read them all. They *all* set the parent up, in one way or another, to take the blame for a child's taking drugs. If a child takes drugs it *must* be something the parents did wrong in either failing to prevent it or in directly causing it. They *all* send parents on deep psychological journeys of self-discovery in search of *their* inadequacies and problems as a means of preventing drug problems in the child. A typical excerpt from a chapter on "Prevention" from one of these books is as follows:

> . . . And the child who watches a parent feel bad about life may feel bad about life himself. And the child or parent who feels bad about his own life is more likely to self-medicate to feel good. Bad feelings are communicated. And bad feelings are a direct, if not scenic, route to drug use."[1]

The chapter goes on at great length asking parents to take a long look into their own "feelings of self-worth." It asks the parent to examine everything imaginable about himself —from "Does his appearance reflect an attitude of self-worth?" to "how he sees himself in relation to the world around him."

After my long, exhaustive, and often depressing journey through the land of Expert Opinion, I was left with a feeling of anger and resentment toward these experts who so blithely malign a group of which I am a proud member— American parents. In my long residency in the drug world I have seen too many cases where one child out of large families—including families in the most drug-blighted areas imaginable—turns to drugs, and the rest do not, to believe there is anything valid or scientific about that kind of reasoning. My own brother took drugs, I never did. My daughter took drugs, my son never did. There is no way I could blame our mom for my brother's taking drugs, nor is there any way that my ex-wife or I can accept the blame for our daughter's decision to take drugs. There are, of course, ex-

---

[1] Beth Polson and Miller Newton, Ph.D., *Not My Kid* (New York: Avon Books, 1985).

treme cases where parents are druggies themselves and the destiny of their unfortunate kids (some born drug addicted) is clearly the fault of the parents. But in the context of our great American drug problem ($200 billion a year), these cases are few and far between.

Besides, what world are these experts living in? Life *is* tough. Many of us are having a hell of a time making it, doing a lot of things we are very unhappy about to survive. *Tough* is part of growing up. Are we supposed to bring our children up by shielding them from "bad feelings"? Or are we better parents if we teach them to cope with negative and bad feelings *without* taking drugs? I could probably write a book on the absurdities of anti–drug-abuse advice given by the experts; but what's the point? In short, one of the most damaging things the experts have done in the area of drug-abuse prevention is to overcomplicate the whole process.

Statistics show that most children with drug problems begin their experimentation between the ages of twelve and thirteen. To prevent their child from becoming one of those statistics, parents should begin taking aggressive preventive measures around the same time that potty training is begun. I can see no reason why drug prevention in young children should be treated any differently than stopping them from playing with matches, playing in traffic, going with strangers, playing with medicine bottles, or any other dangerous and life-threatening activity. And, as any parent knows, to prevent a young child from doing something dangerous to his health and safety requires a level of parental communication no more complicated than a stern warning—and, if the child doesn't listen, a whack on the butt. In fact, the simpler and more direct the communication, the more effective the result.

The drug-abuse prevention program I recommend for

families is short, blunt, and, I'm sure, too simplistic for the tastes of many of the experts. The measures I advocate don't *advise* children that they *shouldn't* take drugs; they *tell* children that the taking of drugs is dangerous and *unacceptable* behavior. They don't *explain* the dangers of taking drugs; they *show* the gruesome damage that drug abuse can inflict on the human body, in as realistic and frightening manner as possible. They don't treat drug abusers as hapless victims; they depict them as the loathsome, selfish, and dangerous slugs that they are. They don't cloud the issues of cause and responsibility for a child's taking drugs, they lay the responsibility of choice directly in the lap of the child.

The Image of the Druggie

It never ceases to amaze me how easily parents can instill prejudice and hatred in their children, based on race, religion, ethnicity, and any other bias the parents might have. If all parents began, today, instilling their young children with a bias against drug users as effectively as they do their other attitudes and prejudices, our next generation of adults would have no drug problem at all.

We must do with the image of drug abusers something similar to what happened in the 1980s with that of smokers. The druggies' image must be such that people wrinkle their noses in disgust at the sight of them, ostracize them publicly, and shun them socially. We must make the offering of "recreational" drugs to a friend among the most vulgar and hateful acts a person might commit, instead of the "cool," "hip," "in" thing to do. If we could enlist Hollywood and the genius of American advertising in *really* going to war against the image of the drug user, we'd have half the battle won. But since we can't, at least for the present, our children's idea of what being a druggie is all about is in our hands; and there is no better opportunity to start building a prejudice against him than in early childhood.

Children should be taught to fear and avoid other children who even hint at experimenting with drugs as they would an infectious disease carrier. They will be the source of your child's first drug experience—not the Medellín Cartel, or the corner drug dealer. Don't lose an opportunity to demonstrate to your children how terribly upset and angry *the bad children* who use drugs make Mommy and Daddy. The evening news, usually rife with stories of celebrities and their involvement with drugs, will provide you with plenty of opportunities to further demonstrate your antidruggie feelings.

The techniques used in shaping their children's attitudes are only limited by the imagination of the parents. One suggestion might be to set up a dollhouse and, using dolls, role-play situations involving "bad children" who use drugs, during which you *show* your child, with much anger and emotion, how you feel about such "terrible" children. Sadly, for parents—considering the uphill battle we face against society's almost unconscious glamorization of the drug world—there can be no such thing as *overdoing* it.

Strong Positive Images

Just as the druggie's image should be, constantly and consistently, presented to children as negatively as possible, strong positive images should be presented to them, as what Mommy and Daddy admire, emphasizing people who think for themselves, are leaders not followers, and above all would never think of doing anything as *awful* as taking drugs.

Frightening Images of Drug Abuse

In today's television age I would recommend that as part of a child's (preschool to six or seven years of age) viewing day, that he or she be exposed to videotapes of graphic and frightening images of the destruction drug abuse wreaks on the human body—*the more frightening the better.* If begun young enough it will instill a healthy knee-jerk reaction *against* even the suggestion by a peer that the child experiment with drugs. If begun *before* a child has the chance to experiment with drugs, this kind of preventive method can be particularly effective.

Take an Active Interest in Your Children

Start as young as possible getting your children into the habit of talking with you about *everything* and anything. No subject should be taboo or unimportant. While our children are still in our care, we cannot afford *not* to be interested in *any* detail of their lives. They should become accustomed to answering all Mommy and Daddy's questions about what they did during the day, who they played with, what the other children's names were, what they said, and so on. Just being interested can lead you to all sorts of amazing discoveries.

In checking on the parents of one of my daughter's friends—with whom she happened to be spending a lot of time—I was shocked to learn that they saw nothing wrong with smoking marijuana with their daughter. The girl has since been in and out of numerous psychiatric and drug-treatment programs. Her life is a living nightmare.

Being a parent is a tough, full-time job. You've got to show your children, clearly and unequivocally, that of all the sorts of behavior considered "unacceptable," drug abuse is one of the worst; that it is so dangerous to their health and happiness that Mommy and Daddy are ever on the alert for it. But that, in the end—no matter how much Mommy and Daddy do—the responsibility for *never* experimenting with drugs is the child's.

Love Is a Two-Way Street

Children should be taught that an important part of love is trusting the person you love not to hurt you; that children have the responsibility of repaying their parents' love with respect, obedience, kindness, and consideration; that once love is abused—even the love of a parent—it can be damaged beyond repair; and, most importantly, that the taking of drugs is one of the worst abuses of a parent's love imaginable.

Prevention in Older Children

If you have a child who is already in his midteens or older and has no involvement with drugs, consider yourself lucky. Take him or her in your arms, hug them, and tell them how much you appreciate the kind of people they are; then keep on doing whatever you've been doing. If you have any reason to believe that your child is already involved with drugs —considering the variety and ferocity of drugs available on the street, no involvement can be considered "minimal"— see the next chapter, "Surviving a Druggie in the Family."

Much of the task of prevention in older children—when it is too late to instill in them an automatic, knee-jerk, fear-disgust reaction to illegal drugs and druggies—involves the undoing of the damage done by the Big Lie, and other misinformation rampant in our society. The child should be approached on his or her intellectual level, by the parent, in an effort to determine what his or her beliefs and feelings are concerning *why* people use drugs. Whenever their ideas vary from the fact that the decision to take drugs—except in extreme cases of child abuse—is both the *choice* and *responsibility* of the child, the child should be corrected.

THE CHOICE IS THEIRS

Parents have to make it clear to their children that the choice of succumbing to druggie-pressure instead of love of family is the child's and *only* the child's; and that it is a choice that may cost him that family.

8

Surviving a Druggie in the Family

The hardest and most painful lesson learned from my twenty-five years as a narcotics agent and my experiences as the father and brother of druggies, is that there is no person more selfish, more depraved, more capable of harm to himself, his family, and his society than the drug user. He has but one concern, from the moment he opens his eyes to face the day to the moment he surrenders to sleep—more important by far than family, love, religion, or country—his drug. And there are none who are in more need of protection from him than those of us made his prisoner by our love—his family.

The suffering of having someone you love transformed into an evil, dangerous stranger, whom you wouldn't trust alone with your silverware, not to mention the soft vulnerable insides of your heart, is one I know well. Through all my years in this sick business, as well as suffering the lives of druggies in my own family, I was compelled to witness and often take part in the suffering of countless innocent families who lost their savings, homes, health, and lives, trying in vain to save druggie loved ones. It is to those of you that I dedicate this section of *Fight Back*.

A COLD, HARD LOOK AT THE DRUGGIE

My dual role in the drug world gave me a unique combination of perspectives. As an undercover narcotics agent I came to know thousands of drug dealers quite intimately. From street-corner pushers to billion-dollar traffickers who controlled their governments, I found that if there was one attitude and feeling that narcotics officers and drug dealers had in common, it was a revulsion against and mistrust of druggies.

Top drug dealers scorn the use of drugs, and those who use them. "Don't get high on your own supply" is the rule, and those who violate it are soon out of business, in jail, or dead. I have worked thousands of undercover cases and managed to penetrate drug organizations all over the world, without once posing as a user. Drug dealers just don't trust them. Even the lowly street dealers tend to shun the druggie as anything but a customer. "Raymond," the head of the PBGs, one of seven hundred drug-dealing street gangs in Los Angeles, expressed the typical street dealer's sentiment when he told a *USA Today* reporter that gang members could sell crack and cocaine, but anyone caught using it was out.[1]

Both cops and dealers know that druggies are incapable of the most basic forms of honesty, trust, morality, and loyalty. And in that world—a world with no courts to resolve business disputes—such lack of character usually leads to death.

[1] Sally Ann Stewart, "Aspiring Break-Dance Group Becomes Drug-Dealing Crips," *USA Today*, 12/7/89.

As an instructor of narcotics undercover tactics and informant handling, I would have been remiss in not telling the thousands of cops and agents I have instructed, "Never use a druggie for an informant, if you can avoid it," and "If you have to pose as a druggie to make a case, the case is too low life to be worth the effort and risk." The druggie is the scum of the very world he created, the lowest of the low, the pariah; the most scorned and the least trusted.

But then, you really shouldn't need cops or drug dealers to warn you about druggies. News stories of them murdering their mothers and fathers, selling their own children into prostitution, and every other bestial crime the imagination can conjure, to get drug money, have become commonplace. A typical story, of many found almost daily in newspapers across the country, was that of a twenty-year-old Long Island, New York, crack addict who killed his grandmother by running her over with a car when she tried to stop him from leaving home after he had stolen $3,000 of his mother's money to buy crack.[1]

Pregnant druggie mothers, by the hundreds of thousands, damage the innocent, unprotected beings in their bellies with the poison of crack and cocaine, and then heartlessly turn the tiny convulsing bodies over to society to care for, while they go out and do it over again.

Yet there were two druggies in my life that I could not have loved more—my brother and my daughter. And their stories—his nineteen-year bout with drug addiction ending with his suicide; her five-year struggle against drug abuse and her victory—form the centerpiece of this section of the book. What I learned taking part in their battles—individual and family actions and attitudes that were effective and

[1] "Crack Killer: Grandma Got in the Way," UPI story, *New York Post,* 7/25/90.

those that were mistaken and ended in failure—was buttressed a thousand times over by the thousands of other cases I took part in and observed.

MY BROTHER'S STORY

(The Two Constants in a "Cure" for Drug Addiction)

It was a cold winter night in 1965 when my mother telephoned me. Her voice was tight with fear. "Michael, please come over. I found something . . . in your brother's room. I want you to tell me what it is."[1] She wouldn't say anything else. She could barely speak. In remembering that phone call now, twenty-five years later, I realize that no words were necessary. I had known instantly what the problem was. Mom and I had both known all along what was happening to David, but had done all we could to deny it. The truth was too painful to accept.

David and I had been very close as kids. Our father had left Mom when we were very young (I was eight, David four), and moved away to another state where we never heard from him again, until we were both in our twenties. On those rough South Bronx streets in those crazy days of fast-changing cultures, languages, colors, smells, and sounds, the appearance of drugs like heroin slipped into our daily lives almost unnoticed. It was a tough time for kids to be on their own as much as David and I were. I was as much of a father and defender as he would ever really have.

Our father—strange man that he was—had left me with a couple of legacies, one of which was "You take care of your little brother. He's your own flesh and blood; and for your

[1] The incident and full story are described in *Undercover*, by Donald Goddard (New York: Times Books, 1988).

own flesh and blood you do anything —even give your life if you have to." The lesson our father taught and promptly forgot, I could not. I probably didn't do a real good job as surrogate dad to my brother, but it wasn't for lack of love. All through our growing-up years, until I joined the air force at eighteen, I had looked out for him, fought his fights for him, and tried to be there for him whenever he needed me. I could not have loved him more.

After my military discharge David and I began to drift apart. I married, continued on to college, and eventually became a federal narcotics agent. David had managed to scrape by in high school, followed by a slow, aimless drift from one trade to another. He always seemed to be kind of restless, vaguely unhappy, and, with the passage of the years, growing more distant and secretive all the time. He lived with Mom and our stepfather—only about a half mile from the apartment I shared with my wife and baby son— yet we rarely saw each other anymore. Back then, I really hadn't noticed the drift. I was too busy, too into my own little world. But I still felt close to him. There was nothing in the world I wouldn't do for him. He was twenty-one years old, but to me he was still my baby brother.

I threw on a leather jacket and as an afterthought shoved my service revolver into my pocket—our Queens, New York, neighborhood had, as of late, become dangerous at night; druggies and muggings were on the rise—and hustled quickly through the half mile of dark streets to my mother's garden apartment. I got there close to midnight. It would be a night I would never forget.

"What is this?" my mother asked, voice cracking through trembling lips, her face pale as chalk, her eyes red rimmed from crying, as I climbed the stairs to her apartment. She held a small black cardboard box, its top still in place, waiting for me to open it. When I did, I stared for a long moment at its contents. I remember the word *evidence* flashing through my mind. Could that have been my first thought? I had just gone through a series of government enforcement schools, and what I was staring at *was* evidence; something I had been methodically taught to believe in with the fervor of a religious fanatic; something you tagged, bagged, and presented to a district attorney as part of a criminal case report; something from another world that I couldn't possibly have any personal relationship with—a filthy, bent hypodermic needle, a blood-crusted syringe operated by a small black rubber squeegie, a dirty spoon, and a couple of glassine packets of white powder—a junkie's "works."

Mom and I both knew what it was. That obscene conglomeration of items from another world didn't even look real in my mom's always spotless apartment. This wasn't supposed to happen to people like us. We were good people, from a long line of good, hardworking people. One of the reasons we had moved away from The Bronx was to escape drugs. God, how could this be happening to us?

I couldn't speak. No words were necessary. It was well past midnight. All I could do was sit listening to the loud ticking of a wall clock, waiting for the sound of my brother opening the door and wondering what I was going to say. The past couple of years careened through my mind, reminding me; accusing me; I had seen it happening all along but had looked the other way.

When I started to cry, it was as though I'd burst a dam that was barely containing both Mom and me. We fell into each other's arms, sobbing. She had found the box, cleaning as usual, on the bottom of my brother's closet, inside a boot. Who in the world, other than our mother, would check shoes in the bottom of a closet for dirty socks? David had to know she would find it. Maybe he wanted to get caught.

Maybe, in spite of everything I knew and was learning about drugs in general and heroin in particular, there was some hope. Maybe he was just dibbing and dabbing, had just been using the stuff for a short time. Maybe there was something we could do.

Maybe.

It was three-thirty in the morning when we heard my brother's key turn in the lock. The moment he saw us he knew. And we all started crying again. When I was able to speak I said, "I love you, but I'm looking at a dead man." I was trying to frighten my brother into waking up. But I was also saying the truth.

Within weeks my brother was in Phoenix House, one of the earliest rehabilitation programs in New York City. He spent about seven months in their Hart Island residence, just off the shore of City Island, The Bronx, with other druggies and ex-druggie counselors, all struggling like hell to help each other. Our whole family used to go out there every weekend and whenever they had parties. It all seemed so hopeful. They had intensive group therapy sessions that were relentless probes into the lives and thoughts of each addict. They exposed their innards for the others to see and critique, all for the purpose of discovering *why* each of them had chosen, in their words, "the coward's" way out of life's problems. They attacked each other's lack of character and shortcomings relentlessly until one or the other broke down in tears. And then they would hold and comfort each other, as if each, by direct contact, was seeking to absorb the strength of the group into his or her own body. They seemed so fervent in their desire to "get straight"; so dedicated and committed to helping each other; so much like hapless victims, that it was hard to see them any other way.

On our trips to the island our family got to know all the kids in treatment and their families. Mom joined a parents' support group. We were all suffering together. My brother had all the love and support a family could give him. There was nothing any of us wouldn't do for him. We learned the group's songs, the group's dance—a proud victory step called "The Phoenix Strut"—and we dared to feel hopeful. David was in such good, caring hands—the hands of experts.

I began to believe that David would be one of the few exceptions to the tragic end that I *knew* drug addiction usually meant. I prayed that what the sick feeling in my gut and my life experiences told me would, in my brother's case, be wrong.

Within months of David's "graduation" from the program he was back on heroin; and, as we learned from the other parents, so were most of the other kids we had met. My brother later told me that on supervised field trips some of the "rehabilitating" addicts had managed to get drugs and bring them back to the island. Many of the same kids who had impressed us with their sincerity and dedication in getting clean were actually still getting stoned. As a narcotics agent I would soon learn that it was all part of the con job that being a druggie is all about. If there is a system— any system—the druggie loves to beat it; and then flaunt it in your face.

It was the beginning of twelve years of torture for my family, especially for Mom, who lived through most of it with him. David went through five rehabilitation programs and, it seemed, every psychologist, psychiatrist, therapist— some of them acknowledged experts with national and even world reputations—and every quack who claimed to be able to "cure" drug addiction.

By late fall of 1975 David was on the methadone program and living with me and my family—my then wife, Liana, and my two children, Keith and Niki (then ten and six years of age, respectively)—in Rockland County, a suburb of New York City. He had been with us a little over a year, during which things seemed to be going pretty good for him. He was holding down a regular job, taking his methadone every day, and paying his bills. Liana and the kids adored him, and he them. He had a real family that cared about him; goals of opening his own business; and a life that once again seemed to be growing brighter and more hopeful every day. But then, as if a huge cloud had covered the sun, everything turned dark.

David suddenly turned secretive and sullen. He disappeared for two and three days at a time, missing work. He always had had nondruggie friends he used to visit in the city. I knew some of them and recognized the others by their names and voices on the phone. Suddenly new names were calling the house, with tight-throated, ragged voices and cryptic messages that were a dead giveaway. I was an undercover narcotics agent. I would have had to bury the top half of my torso to avoid knowing what was going on.

For weeks I agonized over what to do, as my brother's life continued downhill. I didn't have the heart to tell our mom, who had already sacrificed twelve years of her life worrying after him, caring for him, cleaning up after him—and who had been ecstatic at his "progress" and current life—that he was back on heroin again.

Finally we decided that David had to be confronted. By ducking the issue—pretending not to see—we were making the same mistake that had been made when he first started on drugs as a fifteen-year-old. One afternoon, toward the end of October, I woke up late, after working all night. Liana, looking worried, whispered that David was down in his room and had not gone to work. Feeling sick to my stomach I went downstairs for what was to be our final confrontation.

I found my baby brother fully clothed lying on his bed and staring up at the ceiling. There was no pretense at all. He just seemed so tired. He immediately admitted that he was shooting heroin again.

"Why?" I asked. "Even when life is lousy, there is always something new; something different to experience—without drugs. . . . Why? Don't you know we love you; that when you hurt yourself you hurt all of us?"

Then my brother said words that I would hear echoed again and again from druggies over the years to come; words that are often mistaken as a *cause* of drug addiction, when in fact they are just a deadly symptom: "I guess, what I really want to do is kill myself. . . . Only I just don't have the nerve to do it all at once. So I do it a little bit at a time." As he spoke he stared up at the ceiling, unable to look at me. There were tears in his eyes.

My brother understood that he had to leave. I had to draw a line, once and for all, to protect myself and my family, particularly my children, from the nightmare of living with a druggie. I was also sure that I was not doing him any favors by allowing him to continue living with us. I had never asked him to pay rent or anything more than to buy some food once in a while. All I was doing was enabling him to have more money to buy drugs.

I had another motivating factor in asking my brother to leave. By then I had ten years experience in narcotics enforcement and, thanks to my brother, had sought to learn all I could from the experience of every junkie I met. In all the drug addicts who had managed to stay off drugs for more than five years—a number I considered sufficient to indicate a good chance of permanent sobriety—I found what I believed to be two common factors that led to them staying clean:

• *They hit the bottom of life's barrel,* becoming as degenerate as your imagination can conjure; prostituting their bodies, living on the streets like animals, and somehow surviving the experience with their lives and enough of their health to make a comeback.

• *They become obsessed with wanting to cure themselves.* They finally reach a point many have described as being "sick and tired of it," or, "just worn out." Some call it their own "personal bottom." The desire to cure themselves became stronger than their desire for drugs.

My brother had neither hit bottom nor did he have enough *real* desire to cure himself. All junkies *say* they want to be cured. I've heard the typical druggie's lament thousands of times from a thousand druggies: *"Man, I wanna straighten myself out. Man, as soon as I come down, I'm gonna get myself in a program. Man, I'm gonna lick this stuff. Man. Man. Man."* They scream for treatment on demand, and most get it. But what they really want is a rest from the street, a chance to get the size of their habit back under control before they once again turn on their families like dogs biting the hands that feed them, stealing their money and breaking their hearts; and at the same time, destroying whatever sparks of love and decency they might have been rekindling in their own souls, and returning to their *real* love—drugs.

They almost always go back.

David moved to Miami, Florida where, in those years, heroin was a little more difficult to get—we thought. No one considered cocaine much of a problem. (It was four years before our CIA would help the Roberto Suárez cocaine organization take over Bolivia while President Carter's drug advisor, Dr. Peter Bourne, proclaimed to America that cocaine was the "most benign" of drugs.) Our mom went with

David and helped him move his things. Our real father, with whom we had had very little contact during our growing-up years, lived there. He introduced David to people, helped him get a job, and swore he would look out for him. Before long David had a whole new support group of people, as well as us, who loved him and would keep him from hitting life's bottom. Only, no one was doing him any favors.

On February 27, 1977, my baby brother put a gun to his head and ended his life. . . . *I just can't stand the drugs anymore,* said his note.

I received word of my brother's death while teaching a class on narcotics undercover tactics to the Brooklyn district attorney's office investigative staff. On my way home I had to pull my car into a parking area on the Palisades Parkway to try and stop the screaming voices in my head. I sat there for a long time, crying, my mind flooded with the images of David's and my childhood in the South Bronx. Then I thought of my own kids and vowed I would never let it happen to them.

MY DAUGHTER

(Her Victory)

In January 1982, DEA force-transferred me from Buenos Aires, Argentina, to Washington, D.C., because contracts for my death had been issued by Bolivian and Colombian drug dealers. My transfer was quickly followed by a temporary duty assignment to then Vice President Bush's South Florida Task Force; at the same time I was assigned to a long-term deep-cover assignment in Tucson, Arizona, in one of the government's most sensitive drug investigations, Operation Hun.[1] At the same time I was working some smaller undercover cases in Miami and the Carolinas. My official address was a small apartment in the Virginia suburbs of Washington, D.C., but I also kept a one-room apartment in Miami. Most of my time was spent on airplanes shuttling between my assignments. It was not a convenient time to learn that I had another drug war to fight—my daughter's.

When my wife's emergency call came, I was posing as a powerful drug baron, living in a luxury undercover house in the northern foothills of Tucson, with drug dealers from Colombia, Miami, and New York as my invited "guests." She and I had been legally separated during the past several years, with her and the children (Keith, then seventeen, and Niki, thirteen) living in Rockland County, a suburb of New York City.

"I think Niki is taking drugs," said my wife. "I need you here." She was crying. "I can't handle it alone."

That was all she had to say. I still hadn't recovered from my brother's death; not that I ever will. I still can't speak about it without feeling my throat tighten and tears push at the back of my eyes. The thought of my little girl going the way of my brother was too much.

In a hushed voice I told her that I would be there as fast as I could. When I hung up I was crying. One of the drug dealers, a Colombian woman named Anna Tomayo, suddenly entered the room, catching me off guard. I was so taken aback that I told her the truth. The woman, a target of our investigation connected with the infamous Medellín

---

[1] Among the targets of the operation were Luis Arce-Gómez, the minister of the interior of Bolivia, dubbed "The Minister of Cocaine" by the media, and Octavio "Papo" Mejiá, one of the most prolific murderers in Colombia's bloody history. It was probably one of the most important and far-reaching undercover cases of its time, later to become one of the prime examples of the fraud our war on drugs really is.

cartel, hugged me and told me that her daughter also had a terrible drug problem.[1] It was truly a strange moment. I dropped everything. The next night I was on a plane to New York. It was to be the beginning of the most important drug war of my life.

My daughter, Niki, was exhibiting all classic symptoms of a young druggie. Our once bright, cheery little girl had suddenly become secretive, dark, brooding, and given to wild, screaming tantrums. She had new, equally secretive friends that my wife knew little about. The innocent stuffed animals and rock and roll posters in her room had been replaced with drug symbols, slogans, psychedelic lights, and posters. Her school grades had deteriorated markedly, and —to my wife's shock—she had been absent from school for about half the term and had been forging her mother's handwriting on "excuse" notes.

My baby girl had undergone the kind of rapid and dramatic change that during the years of my childhood might have been confused with demonic possession, but nowadays is easily recognized as typical druggie behavior. She had also become extremely violent. She was too strong and— especially when under the influence of drugs—uncontrollable for her mother to handle. Whenever my wife made any attempts at controlling her or confronting her with her behavior, she would react physically, by shoving, cursing, and breaking and throwing things.

Under my strict orders my son, a normally gentle and easygoing seventeen-year-old with a black belt in karate, tried to stay out of any problems between his mother and sister. Even though it would usually take me as much as twenty-four hours to get to New York during the many

[1] Anna Tomayo was one of the eleven extradited from Colombia in 1989. The whole story of Operation Hun will be told in a forthcoming book.

crises my daughter was provoking, I did not want my son playing the role of father. It was a mistake that had been made with my brother. Even so, witnessing his mother treated that way was too much for him. He finally exploded and went after Niki. Within hours I was on a plane to New York. Something had to be done before a tragedy occurred. Through tears my son said, "I just couldn't take seeing *anyone* treat Mom like that." I cried with him. We were being devoured by my daughter's choice of life-style, and it just wasn't fair.

There was, as is typical with druggies, no reasoning with Niki. It was as if she were angry at the world and had decided to take it out on her own body and her family. Her articulation of that anger never amounted to more than a screaming accusation, "What the hell do you care what happens to me, you're traveling all over the world?" or "All I want to be is left alone!" "What family? I haven't got a family."

A drug "expert" would have had a field day with us. As parents we were guilty of all the classic things that they claim "cause" children to turn to drugs. We had a rough, unhappy marriage that, at times, had exploded right in front of the children, showering them with plenty of "bad feelings." And being an undercover narcotics agent did not leave me with much time to be at home. And then, finally, came the separation.

But at the same time we had always smothered our kids in love. No matter where I was, I made sure I was always in contact with them; that they had all the things they needed; and that they didn't doubt for a second that they had a father they could depend on. Wasn't I proving it by being there? My son was growing up under the same conditions as his sister and had never touched drugs. By then I had known plenty of kids growing up under the worst conditions imaginable, who had not turned to drugs.

What right did she have to do this to us?

Whenever my daughter pulled one of her disappearances I would drop everything and fly to New York from wherever I happened to be, and with gun and badge search for her and her connection. I was once again living a nightmare. At one point I pulled a one-man raid of a house party with a couple of hundred kids in attendance. I charged past and through groups of stoned and semistoned teenagers, lying on the front lawn, in bushes, and strewn around the house like human logs, looking for my daughter. One glassy-eyed kid stood in the middle of the living room staring at an object between his fingertips as though it were the stub of a marijuana joint. I snatched it out of his hands, drew my badge, and was about to announce the arrest of everyone present when I realized I was holding a moth.

"Who is that?" someone whispered.

"I'm Niki Levine's father," I said. "And you can bet your little druggie asses that wherever she's invited I'm going to be right behind her."

I didn't do much for my daughter's popularity, and likewise was not doing too well in getting her to change her druggie ways. She was a constant truant and was now getting into trouble at every turn. When she and another girl had a fistfight at a local swimming pool, ending with the girl attacking my daughter with a knife, a local cop who knew me pulled me aside and said, "Mike, the people your daughter is staying with are garbage; they're degenerate druggies." Those words from a fellow law-enforcement officer were like a dagger in my heart, *garbage, degenerate druggies . . . my daughter.*

My daughter's situation was turning critical. The limit to our love and patience was coming closer and my baby girl was barely fifteen. Her situation had become so bad that I had enough evidence for DEA to grant me a "compassionate" (hardship) transfer back to New York. At least I would be saving on my immense airline bills. I gathered my things from Miami and Virginia into a rented van and headed back to New York and a final showdown.

My transfer back to New York seemed to inflame things further. I was placed in charge of a street enforcement group working around the clock on some of the toughest and most bizarre drug cases in my career, and at the same time having to constantly drop everything and race home to get my daughter out of one fix after the other.

From the beginning I was determined not to make the mistake that had been made with my brother; that of unconditional love. A druggie can, unmindful of the blight he is causing, guzzle down a reservoir full of love without returning a single drop. In all my years in the drug world I had never heard of a druggie repaying unconditional love with anything but the ugliest forms of treachery.

It is *always* this way. Ask the parent or loved one of any druggie.

Our alternatives, while painful, were quite clear. As much as we loved our daughter there had to be a limit to how far we would go in tolerating her behavior. There had to be a very definite psychological line drawn, the crossing of which would signify that, as much as we loved her, she was simply no longer capable of returning that love—a point beyond which we would have to put her out of our lives to protect ourselves.

I guessed that reaching our limit would be signaled by subtle psychological changes, as happened with my brother —a numbing of the insides against a murderous pain that never goes away; a strengthening of resolve; a deadening of emotion—and then it would be over. My daughter—once the source of so much joy, and now so much pain—would no longer occupy that vulnerable spot in our hearts. She would have banished herself to a cold, isolated spot in our family psyche, where we could tolerate the tragic end we knew was coming. There would be no more choices. She would no longer be welcome in our family. I would have to do as I had done with my brother—ask her to pack up and leave our home. These were all thoughts of mine which I made certain my daughter was aware of. The choice of pushing us to that limit, as I kept reminding her after each ugly incident, was all hers.

Of course, the last-ditch hope was that the threat of reaching that limit would awaken her and cause her to at least *want* to stop taking drugs. For this final hope to work, the threat not only had to be perceived as real, it had to *be* real. Any parent of a druggie who issues a single threat that is not carried out lessens his chances of ever effecting change. If you're in the habit of issuing empty threats, a druggie will swallow you up whole.

Just after her sixteenth birthday Niki was at her worst. It seemed that supporting her and allowing her to live at home any further was both enabling and encouraging her self-destruction. It was my brother's story all over again. I consulted attorneys and began the necessary legal moves to petition the courts to have our daughter treated as an adult and put out of our home. If she wanted to continue her life as a druggie she would have to do it on her own. We were no longer her parents—not by our choice, but by her treatment of us.

As we began to take action, I made sure our daughter was constantly reminded of the thoughts and feelings motivating us, and that, until the moment she was forced to leave our home, her destiny was still in her hands. To stop the process, we had only one condition: *no drugs.*

On the day I was to go to an attorney's office to begin the proceedings, I told Niki, "Honey, what it all comes down to is a choice of love. If I love you enough to feed you, clothe you, spend most of my waking hours worrying about you, and turn my whole life upside down on a moment's notice to try and help you—and you don't love me enough to care how much you're hurting me—then to protect myself, I have to go through with this. It broke my heart, but I did it with Uncle David. And I never saw him again. And now I've got to do the same with my little girl."

I will always remember her face when I said those words. I think it was the first time she was aware of the place she had brought us to; and most importantly, of how *real* my words were. As father and daughter we were one step from the finish line. We both realized it and both started crying. It was the first show of feelings I had seen in her in two years. I took her in my arms and for the first time began to understand how lonely she was.

The change in Niki was a gradual one. At first she did just enough to forestall the petition. It was tough for a sixteen-year-old girl, overnight, to go from being part of the so-called "cool," "hip," drug-taking, partying "in" crowd, to having enough will and strength of character to be her own person. I had made arrangements with her school that they contact me immediately if there were any problems with her behavior or attendance. She had to keep either her mother or me advised of where she was at all times. On school nights there was no going out, and on the weekends she had to be home by midnight.

During the next two years there were occasional relapses —short-lived returns to the old crowd, lies, tears, and promises never to do it again—but her overall behavior, while not an immediate about-face, was constantly improving. I could see that my little girl *was* trying and that was good enough for me.

Throughout the whole process of recovery I was relentless in exposing Niki to my negative feelings about druggies and the choice they made by choosing drugs and druggie "friends" as incapable of love as they were, over their families. I would come home daily, armed with a "million" sick druggie stories from my job, further emphasizing the low rung they occupied on life's ladder, and what a terribly "uncool" thing it was to be a druggie. I tried to get her to think clearly about the kind of people she had chosen as her intimates, and how little they really cared about anything in life —least of all her.

By the time Niki graduated high school, just before her eighteenth birthday, she had a new boyfriend with whom she had begun her own business. The transformation was incredible and watching it happen was the greatest experience of my life.

It is now more than five years since my daughter has had a drug problem and we are now very close, as we always will be. When I began the writing of this book I asked her what she thought it was that had convinced her to change. She thought for a long moment and said: "I just didn't want to lose you as a father."

It was a moment I will never forget.

Niki had made a choice of love. And I am so proud of her.

Thank God.

My two and a half decades of total immersion in the drug world have taught me that my family's drug problems were in no way unique. By the time I was faced with my daughter's problem, my personal and professional life had forced me through a relentless and brutal education into the reality of what being a druggie was all about, and made me immune to the kind of denial that most parents (and loved ones) of drug abusers are usually guilty of. Before I realized what was happening, the father in me had stepped aside so that the more practical narcotics agent could take over. Armed with the practical knowledge in this book, I believe any parent or loved one of a druggie can do the same . . . must do the same. If you are unfortunate enough to love a druggie . . . no matter what you do, you're in for a very rough ride. So brace yourself.

MANAGING AND SURVIVING THE DRUGGIE IN THE FAMILY

Before writing my opinions on managing and surviving the drug abuser in the family, I read as many expert opinions on the subject as I could.

I found that nearly all of them advise parents and families of druggies to deposit their drug problem in the hands of "experts." The role of the family is always subordinate to, and dependent on, the advice of these experts. The destruction of the rest of the family, while the treatment of the druggie is going on, is hardly ever considered. Most of these experts gear their therapeutic methods toward what they perceive are the root causes of drug abuse—everything from lack of economic opportunity and racism to dysfunctional families, problems of self-esteem, and sexual identification— and don't focus enough on the fact that it is simply wrong and self-destructive to solve *any* problems with self-administered drugs. The families are also advised to seek "professional help" in order to identify in what ways *they* are to blame for their loved ones' turning to drugs. What has never ceased to amaze me about all of us who have suffered living with and loving a druggie is our unflinching willingness to leave our problem in the hands of these experts, in spite of their almost three decades of total failure.

A Choice of Love

The most important factor in helping a drug abuser to save himself is motivating him to genuinely *want* to stop taking drugs. And that is most effectively accomplished by those closest to him, the family, in a very simple direct way —through a choice of love. *If we are ripping our lives apart and breaking our hearts to help you, you must prove yourself worthy of that kind of love . . . or lose it.*

One of the more interesting and revealing books I read in researching this section of *Fight Back* was written by Ken Barun, an ex-addict who had not only recovered from drug addiction but went on to a distinguished career in government and then private industry.[1] In the book Mr. Barun described a key moment leading to his full recovery, when his parents—after suffering through years of his drug addiction, during which they supported him with all their resources and the kind of love only parents can understand— finally threw him out of their home.

> *"Forcing me out on the streets was the kindest, most loving act my parents could have performed,"* wrote Ken Barun. *"It was what eventually led me to straighten out my life."*

Ken Barun was given a choice of love that would lead to his *really* wanting to be drug free. And once the motivation was there the work of the experts was made easy—if not

[1] Ken Barun and Philip Bashe, *How to Keep the Children You Love Off Drugs* (New York: The Atlantic Monthly Press, 1988).

unnecessary. Without that motivation you can expect many years of many visits to many experts—none of whom are afraid to charge handsomely—and to be told many times that "relapse is an expected part of recovery."

The following are what I have found to be the most important dos and don'ts in helping to motivate a druggie in the family to want to stop taking drugs; and, most importantly, to help the rest of the family to survive the experience:

1. Do *not* ignore the obvious signs

When we discovered that my brother had been using heroin for five years, suddenly everything was clear. The signs that he had been using drugs had been there all along, only we had done everything possible to deny them. It was just too painful and frightening for us to accept evidence that had been right there before our eyes for years.

My brother a low-life, slug junkie? Never! No way! Well, sure, he's been listless, distant, and moody lately. He works hard. So what if his nose is running, his eyes are always red, he's lost weight, and looks a little unkempt; when you work real hard you let yourself get run down.

The experts call it "denial," and it is one of the most common and consistent phenomena in the families of drug abusers. What happens most often is that the drug abuser is finally confronted when his behavior becomes so destructive that not even the blindest member of the family can avoid seeing it. In most cases, by that time, he is in the third stage of drug abuse, and the most difficult to combat.

If you have a family member exhibiting one or more of the following symptoms, you probably have a druggie on your hands (the more symptoms exhibited, the more likely that the cause is drug abuse):

a. Changes in mood and behavior, such as lying and secretiveness; severe mood swings with inappropriate, sometimes irrational, fits of anger and hostility; a general increase in irritability; or, a notable dullness, lack of energy and motivation; difficult-to-explain absences; a sudden loss of outside interests and hobbies. Any relatively sudden change of behavior should be suspect.

b. Signs of physical deterioration such as memory lapses, difficulty in concentration, slurred and sometimes incoherent speech, unhealthy and unkempt appearance, bloodshot eyes, dilated pupils, chronically congested nasal passages, and nosebleeds.

c. Hostility when you broach the subject of drugs.

d. Trouble with the police or other authorities.

e. Trouble in school such as truancy, a dramatic change in grades, arguments and fights with other students and teachers.

f. Possession of drug-related paraphernalia—cocaine-spoon jewelry, rolling paper, tiny plastic bottles, metal spoons, hypodermic needle, scales, small butane torches, or objects that look as though they might serve as pipes. (They will always tell you: *"All the kids wear it. It's just a cool thing to wear, Mom. It means nothing."*—Don't believe it!)

g. Possession of any unexplained pills, peculiar plants, butts, seeds, leaves, or powder.

h. Possession of drug-culture literature, magazines, posters, slogans on clothing or schoolbooks.

i. Possession of large amounts of unexplained money.

2. Do not delay or avoid confrontation

If you suspect that your child, or a family member, is abusing drugs, the worst thing you can possibly do is avoid or delay confronting him, or her, with the problem. The earlier the problem is caught and addressed, the better the chances are for cure and rehabilitation. If there is one thing all the experts seem to agree on, it is that the worst thing you can do with a drug-abuse problem in the family is *not* confront it.

3. The confrontation

(Simplify the issue—it's a choice of love)

The confrontation should never occur while the child (or other family member) is under the influence of drugs, and should be as calm and objective as possible. For a lot of people it is going to require the exercise of a lot of self-control and the stifling of emotions that are pushing you toward hysteria—but it must be done. Whether the child admits to drug use or not—it is rare for a druggie to admit it, even when caught red handed—restrictions must immediately be imposed that will assure *you* that the child is clean. A druggie's word is *never* to be trusted.

As calmly as possible you must bring the issue down to what it really is—a choice of love—and keep it there, no matter what the druggie says. It is your *love* that has made you watchful and suspicious. It is your *love* that forces you to tolerate the kind of behavior you have noted. And it is your *love* that is behind your imposing restrictions that would stop your child from destroying himself along with the rest of the family.

This should be followed by a line that you will repeat many times: **"My love will only endure so much, until I have to protect myself and the rest of the family from you."**

Point out what common knowledge it is that druggies are totally incapable of love, and that it is a simple choice—the love of his or her family, or drugs—and that once it is obvious that the choice is clearly drugs, the drug abuser will lose his or her family.

The druggie must be constantly reminded, throughout all the family turmoil that will most surely evolve out of his drug use, that in the end, his destiny is in his hands; that forcing his family to act in order to defend itself is *his* choice.

Inevitably, either through confrontation, arrest, or some other means, a drug abuser and his parents (or family) will come to a point where there are no more pretexts or denials, and his behavior is out in the open. Once caught, in most cases, the druggie will be remorseful and willing to promise anything. The war has begun.

4. Consult physician

If the drug abuser is addicted to hard drugs and needs to be physically withdrawn, a physician must be consulted at once. The withdrawal from some types of drugs is extremely dangerous (see Appendix I) and should not be attempted without expert medical advice. If it is decided that the drug abuser is to remain home, restrictions should be imposed immediately. If he or she is interned in a hospital for physical withdrawal (usually ninety days), restrictions must be imposed immediately on returning to the home.

5. Impose restrictions

The idea of imposing restrictions is to make it as physically difficult as possible for the drug abuser to persist in his ways. There can be no ifs, ands, or buts about it; the child (or any drug abuser in the family) must know that *if* he is going to continue living in the home, there will be *no possibility* of using drugs. The suggested restrictions are as follows (while the list refers to *child,* the restrictions should be the same for any drug abuser in the family):

a. Control and curfew. In general, the child's whereabouts, what they are doing and with whom (names of friends, phone numbers, and so on), must be known at *all* times. Any unexplained absences should ring an alarm bell. An acceptable hour must be set for the child to be home on *every* evening, with no exceptions. The idea of the curfew is twofold: First, it is a means of control and security. Second, it is a way of telling your child that until he reaches adulthood, his life is *not* his to control. The law says that parents are responsible for their children until (in most states) the age of eighteen. Children have no *right* to the control of their lives. It's a privilege they must earn.

b. Drug testing. I would insist that the child agree to drug testing, whenever his or her behavior becomes suspect. This is especially important where there are other siblings in the family. Druggies are known to turn their brothers and sisters on to drugs. The safety of the other children in the family must not be compromised.

6. Be an aggressive investigator. Druggies never tell the truth and have no honor. Those are some hard facts to accept about your own child or loved one, but if they are doing what you suspect them of doing, then accepting their word or promise about *anything* can be a serious error. It bears repeating that part of being a druggie is conning, jiving, and beating the system. For parents to be sure that they aren't conned or jived, I would recommend the following:

a. Become as knowledgeable as possible about the drug world—drugs of abuse and related symptoms (see Appendix I), drug-culture paraphernalia and jargon (see Glossary).

b. Watch your child carefully for all signs of drug abuse.

c. Call the school and arrange that someone in the family be *immediately* notified of all absences or lateness.

d. Talk to the parents of friends to learn if they are experiencing similar trouble and—if they are of a like mind—to create a support group. During my daughter's war on drugs I met parents who were beyond belief, whose reactions ranged from total deaf-and-dumb denial, to actually smoking dope with their kids. So be selective about which parents your child knows you are involved with. You can end up looking like a boob, and that is the last thing you want to happen.

e. Periodically search the child's room for evidence of drug abuse (narcotic paraphernalia, et cetera). There are now sprays available from various testing companies that can tell if drugs have been on any given surface—get them.

f. Make arrangements, when the child's behavior is suspect, for periodic drug testing through your family physician.

g. Hide a tape recorder and turn it on when the druggie is at his destructive worst. Later, when he is straight, play it for him.

7. Treatment and rehabilitation programs

If your child or loved one is properly motivated to quit drugs, almost any qualified treatment program will work. The question of whether or not a child should enter a program should be left up to the child. My daughter, for example, did not want to enter a program. Once she had made up her mind that she was finished with drugs, she felt that being lumped together with a lot of druggies was the environment she wanted most to avoid. She did fine on her own (with strong family support). My brother went through every treatment and rehabilitation program available and never really stopped taking drugs. One of the important differences between the two was in the motivation and desire to quit, without which no program will work.

This does not mean that if your child wants to enter a program or undergo treatment by a professional that *any* program or professional will do. On the contrary. There is an incredible variety of licensed programs and professionals available for the treatment of substance abuse, and some of them are pretty wacky. My brother, for example, attended something called Scream Therapy just before committing suicide.

8. Select a therapist or treatment program carefully

Before allowing your child to enter a program or be treated by anyone, you must first thoroughly satisfy yourself, by visiting and attending therapy sessions and/or interviewing the professionals involved, that their methods and practices are not potentially harmful, and are in accordance with what you have been teaching your child. Specifically, the parent should assure himself that the potential therapist is in agreement with the following:

a. That the taking of self-administered drugs as a solution to *any* problem is wrong. There are a dismaying number of so-called experts who do not agree with this. If a psychologist tells you, "Well, Mrs. Smith, taking a marijuana joint every now and then really isn't so terrible," thank him for his time and look for another therapist.

b. That the child, and the child alone, is responsible for his choice in taking drugs.

c. That parents—not children—are responsible for, and in control of, children's actions and lives, at least until "legal" adulthood.

d. That the taking of drugs is a violation of parents' trust and an extreme abuse of their love.

e. That relapse should *not* be an accepted part of a treatment and rehabilitation program.

Once satisfied that the treatment is in accordance with your beliefs or that the therapist is someone you want your child exposed to, bring the child on a visit to see how he or she feels about being there. If there are any negative feelings, discuss them; if they cannot be reconciled, move on to the next program—there are plenty out there.

210 MICHAEL LEVINE

9. Stay on top of the treatment

Once your child enters a treatment program, *never,* I repeat, *never* leave their fate in the hands of experts. Most families of druggies breathe a deep sigh of relief once they manage to get their loved one into a program—any program—and off their hands. They kid themselves into thinking they did the right thing and that their responsibility—thank God—has been transferred to the experts. This attitude is probably one of the primary reasons that treatment and rehabilitation programs are experiencing so many relapses and failures. To insure that your child gets the most out of whatever treatment program you've chosen, with the fewest problems, you must:

a. Take part in and be aware of *everything* going on in the program and how your child feels about it, keeping a keen eye and ear out for problems. Days before my brother's suicide, friends of his reported that he had spoken of "something" that had happened during a therapy session that had upset him greatly.

b. Be sure that your child is mindful of the fact that he, or she, is in treatment to get *support* in overcoming a problem, the solution of which is the child's responsibility—not the therapist's. Druggies love to blame their problems and failures on someone else, and society, with its phony war on drugs, is catering to their self-deception.

"Man, you gotta stop them people from sending drugs over here. They're killing us," said an obviously stoned caller during a radio interview I did in Atlanta, Georgia.

"Sir," I said, "you're not a victim. You're a suicide."[1]

c. While your child is in a treatment program, reinforce the idea that—while he is trying to help himself—you will leave no stone unturned in supporting him, but that

[1] *Talk Back with Joe Walker* show, Atlanta, Georgia, March 7, 1990.

that kind of love is *only* merited with love in return; and that the choice of drugs over the love of one's parents is one only the druggie can make, on his own.

10. Your limit and the consequences

This is the toughest part of handling a druggie in the family and the most necessary. How much of the horror of living with and loving a druggie a family can suffer is a question only the family itself can answer.

I was not sure how much I could endure with my own brother and daughter; *they* answered the question for me. An inner alarm sounded that told me that tolerating their lives an instant longer was not only going to destroy our family, it was also *helping* them toward their own destruction.

When that alarm sounds is not something that can be predicted. You will be at your wit's end at your job or profession, having exhausted the patience of your associates by constantly having to break up your workday to handle emergencies; money, jewelry, and other valuables will constantly be missing from your home; you will be receiving strange calls at all hours of the night; you will become a familiar face at the school, social-service offices, courts, and the police department; you will have gone deep into debt to pay lawyers and high-priced therapists; and your family life will have degenerated to one hateful, screaming—even physically violent—confrontation after the other.

Suddenly you will realize that the druggie has stolen the joy from the lives of everyone in the family; and that the pain of once and for all separating him from your lives, while excruciating, is the only salvation left.

The druggie has made that choice—not you.

If there is any hope left for him, it will be in learning what it is to face life *without* the family whose love he was so careless with.

Conclusion

The way our politicians and drug-war leaders have chosen to fight this war on drugs reminds me of an old idiot joke from my South Bronx childhood that went: Why did the idiot look for his wallet across the street, when he lost it on this side? The answer: Because there's more light over there.

While our leaders continue to fight their failed, wasteful, and deadly drug war all over the globe, right here in the United States millions of arrests are made each year of felons showing traces of drugs in their systems;[1] tens of thousands of drug-related incidents involving airline pilots, bus drivers, schoolteachers, police, and other members of the most life-and-safety-sensitive positions in our society occur; and millions of druggies continue spending hundreds of billions of dollars, fattening the coffers of the drug economy

[1] According to the *Narc Officer,* the official publication of the International Narcotic Enforcement Officers' Association Inc., July 1990 edition, up to 1.7 million arrests were made in sixty-one major cities, of felons showing traces of cocaine in their systems.

and adding fuel to the fires of violence spreading throughout our land—and virtually nothing is done to stop them.

It defies logic that after all this time, all these wasted lives and dollars, our leaders have not even looked at a system of mandatory treatment and rehabilitation that would give these felons a choice between facing the justice system or voluntarily enlisting in a mandatory lifetime treatment program; a program that would feature frequent testing, making it impossible that these drug users remain free while using drugs; a program that would effectively dry up the drug market and finally put an end to the madness.

All is not lost, however, because if our leaders won't do it, we citizens can do it without them.

My quarter of a century in this so-called "drug war" has convinced me that a grass-roots effort of focusing the immense power of the citizens' and community organizations across America against the drug abuser can show our bureaucrats and politicians how to end our drug problems as rapidly and effectively as Japan and China did it. Unfortunately, at this writing, that power is being misdirected and wasted to an almost criminal degree.

On June 23, 1990, I attended an all-day conference that gave me all the ammunition I needed. The conference, sponsored by the New York Alliance for a Drug-Free City, the umbrella group for the ten thousand neighborhood, block, and building associations representing well over a million New York City residents involved in trying to "fight drugs" in their communities, was also attended by representatives of citizens' coalitions from Baltimore, Philadelphia, Boston, and other major East Coast cities. Its purpose was to discuss difficulties encountered by citizens' groups in organizing and "fighting drugs." It was an opportunity for me to get a firsthand look at why a significant number of well-meaning, dedicated, and well-organized Americans were failing to have any effect in stopping, or even slowing, drug trafficking in their own communities.

Before going any further in describing the events that followed, I want to make it perfectly clear that I in no way want any of my observations to be taken as criticisms of the wonderful well-meaning people I met at this meeting. If there is any hope in our war against drug abuse, it is they. What follows is strictly a description of what I saw and heard.

My first thought on entering the large, crowded auditorium was that I was seeing quite a different picture from what our politicians were presenting—the problem *has* the attention of the American public.

The conference was begun with a short speech by Dr. Lucy Friedman (Ph.D., social psychology). Dr. Friedman had just completed her duties as executive director of a study entitled "Report and Recommendations to the Mayor on Drug Abuse in New York City," and had some startling statistics to report. In New York City:

• There are half a million drug addicts (considered a conservative estimate).

• Twenty-eight drug-addicted babies are born every day.

• Eighty percent of all felony arrests tested positive for drugs.

• A half-billion dollars is spent yearly on drug-related law enforcement.

• It cost $200 million a year to prosecute drug felony charges.

I thumbed through a copy of the report as Dr. Friedman spoke, wondering about "The Great American Change of Mind" Drug Czar William Bennett had been telling us about. It was immediately apparent that the report was similar to the already failed national drug policy, in that it recommended—as remedies for the massive drug problems —many of the same types of broad-based programs for law enforcement, education, treatment, research, criminal justice, and a myriad of community pilot projects, et cetera already recommended by the federal government.

Skimming over the bold print of the report's recommendations, I noticed that there did not seem to be a single change in philosophy, approach, or tactics from any of the hundreds of similar reports I'd seen during my twenty-five years in the drug war. It was just more of the same—*much, much more.* We were still at war against *drugs.*

The other thing I noticed, glaringly absent from the 117-page report, was any indication of an effort to control the drug consumer. He was still being perceived as a victim who was being *offered* treatment, when and if *he* wanted it. The report recommended that significant funding be directed at treatment and rehabilitation. It said that in fiscal year 1991, for the first time since New York's scandal-ridden Addictions Services was dismantled, the city would be contracting drug-treatment providers directly.

Unil the next scandal, I thought, my head reeling with the test of honesty the bureaucrats, politicians, and treatment providers would be facing, having all those hundreds of millions of taxpayer dollars to dole out for the treatment of druggies. I also noted that there was nothing in the report indicating that the "treatment providers" would have to account for a cure rate. Of course not! Since the "experts" in the drug-treatment industry—now one of our nation's larger profit-making enterprises—claim that relapse is part of the rehabilitation process, how do we measure a cure rate? How can we tell if they are ineffective? How can we tell if they are frauds? The trouble is, we can't. All we *can* say is that there are *no* treatment or rehabilitation programs successful enough to make *any* noticeable impact on the national problem.

When Dr. Friedman had completed her address (questions were not permitted in order to save time for the important problem-solving workshops to follow), I collared her on the way out of the auditorium.

"I'm an ex–narcotics agent," I said. "I'm writing a book about what citizens' groups might do to more effectively combat drug abuse. Does your report recommend anything new? I mean *different* from past approaches to the problem?"

She thought for a moment and answered an honest, "No, not really."

Maybe Dr. Friedman was rushed and didn't have much time to consider her answer; I don't know. It didn't really matter, though, because a thorough study of the report buttressed my first impression: there truly *wasn't* anything new. Three quarters of a billion dollars for *one* year in just *one* city was about to be spent on the same kinds of enforcement, prevention, and treatment programs that have been failing for almost three decades.

The report also indicated that New York State's Governor Cuomo had asked the state legislature to budget $1.43 billion for the drug war. The figures bubbled in my brain. I tried to imagine them multiplied by all the other state, city, county, and town "antidrug" budgets across the country. I added the $10.40 billion the federal government has budgeted for this year, and the figure I came up with for American taxpayer money wasted in the drug war was both frightening and demoralizing. It also occurred to me that, as a nation, we may be spending more on fighting the drug war than we are on drugs; and that it would probably take a team of mathematicians and computer experts to figure out where federal spending ended and state, city, and local municipality spending began. But then, what difference does it make? The money is all coming out of one set of pockets—ours. I wondered when we would finally hit the bottom of the Great American Pocketbook.

After the opening remarks the audience separated and headed for assigned classrooms where they were to discuss the difficulties and obstacles confronting them in fighting "drug problems" in their buildings, neighborhoods, and communities, and, perhaps, discover some solutions. I found myself in a large classroom along with about thirty people, most of whom were either leaders or representatives of citizens' organizations. The hope, energy, and enthusiasm I felt in that room was inspiring.

We were next broken down into three smaller study groups, with each group given the assignment of, first, listing the primary *causes* of the drug-abuse problem, then, the *difficulties* faced by citizens in organizing and combating the causes, and finally, the possible *solutions* to these problems.

Undaunted I joined my assigned study group. I had long given up hope of doing anything meaningful to change things through bureaucrats and politicians. If there was any hope in this so-called war on drugs, it lay with people like these. Our group leader, an energetic young lady, gathered us in one corner of the room and stood, chalk poised, before a blackboard. She began by asking for volunteers to list the "causes" of our drug problems. A man raised his hand and said, "drugs." Our leader dutifully printed "drugs" at the top of the list. More hands were raised and the Causes list continued: "drug dealers," was added; then "racism," "poverty," "lack of opportunity," "landlords," "corruption," "greed," "money," and "politics." Finally, there were no more hands raised.

"Are there any more causes?" asked the leader. "Let's just stick to causes." The members of the group all looked at one another. I fought the old P.S. 67 instinct—learned at the end of my fifth-grade teacher Mrs. Shapiro's yardstick—to raise my hand.

"Okay," said the leader, "let's move on to difficulties."

I looked around the room at the blackboards of the other three study groups. Under the "Causes" lists I could see everything from "politics" to *"glasnost,"* but no one—absolutely no one—had mentioned *The User.*

Could this be? I wondered. *Can our politicians and bureaucrats, in their single-minded, militarized war on drugs, have us so brainwashed that we cannot see the forest for the trees?*

After each of the subgroups had finished compiling its list of causes, difficulties, and solutions, we reconvened in the larger group to discuss our findings. In the dialogue that followed, I was once again astounded at the complete absence from the discussion—which included every imaginable theory about our drug problems, including some pretty bizarre ones—of the druggie. There was not a hint of his culpability, or the slightest suggestion that the key for the effective battle against drugs by citizens' groups *might* be the focusing of their considerable resources against him. The idea was never even considered.

I slipped out of the room near the end of the discussion and started peeking into the other half-dozen classrooms, full of leaders and representatives of citizens' groups. Luckily, none of the blackboards had been erased yet. The "Causes" lists were all the same. Not one included a single mention of the druggie; who apparently, in the consensus of the leadership of a good portion of the East Coast's citizenry against drugs, was blameless. The primary causes of our drug problems were "drugs" and "drug dealers"—in any order, followed by everything else one's imagination could conjure; minus, of course, that poor, hapless victim, the druggie.

I was incredulous. I felt like a scientist who had suddenly discovered positive proof of the validity of all his theories. I began to snap pictures of the blackboards. Who would believe this?

The afternoon session was even more enlightening. Once again, in a group workshop devoted to "Police and Community Relations," I listened to descriptions of nightmarish living conditions for which the blame was again attributed to drugs and the dealers. All the community organization activities, as described, were focused on either supplying the police with information *about* drug dealers, or, trying to get more and better police action *against* drug dealers. There were a couple of cops in civilian clothes in the audience, who—I guessed from their attitudes—had been assigned to attend the meeting as symbols of the department's, or some politician's, concern. From time to time I noticed the knowing, half-smiling "cops' looks" that passed between them— looks that spoke eloquently of the futility of the whole subject. At that moment I could not have felt more empathy for the good people of these citizens' groups.

Finally two neighborhood group leaders, who claimed to have scored successes in their drug wars, took seats in front of the room to describe what they had done. Both happened to be black men from druggie-ravaged neighborhoods in Brooklyn.

The first, a powerful and impressive man named Ice Foster, told of his twelve-year battle with the "drug dealers" of his building. "It was either them or me," he said, and there was no braggadocio in his words or manner—he meant what he said. Twelve years earlier Mr. Foster, whose fortitude can in no way be overstated, had moved into a building that had 150 apartment units, 21 of which were inhabited by drug dealers.

He defied them.

He organized the cowed and terrified tenants into an action group, and instilled in them an attitude of togetherness that let the drug dealers know, as he put it: "If they messed with one of us, they were messing with all of us." All the tenants were given alarm whistles and practiced fall-out drills rushing to each other's aid, and "Foster's war" began.

Mr. Foster described several frightening confrontations between his tenants' organization and the dealers, including one where three "little old ladies" confronted one of the drug dealers in the hallway, flailing at him with brooms. The encounter ended with every tenant in the building rushing to the women's aid. Ice Foster had "war stories" ad infinitum. The group listened in respectful silence to all the obstacles he had had to overcome. He was truly inspirational; a brave man; a heroic man. I got so caught up in the stories that I had almost forgot my role as observer and documenter. I was envisioning Ice in the Drug Czar's post, and the tough-talking Dr. Bennett in a Brooklyn tenement fighting the drug dealers. I could contain myself no longer. I raised my hand to speak.

"How did it all end?" I asked.

"We finally got all the dealers out of the building," said the huge man, with deserved pride. "There's not a one left."

"Where are they now?"

"Outside on the street," he said.

I kept my mouth shut. There was no way I was going to diminish this man's twelve-year struggle. Besides, I had a sneaking suspicion that if he and Dr. Bennett *had* changed places, the drug dealers would still control the building. But looking at Ice Foster, I could not help but think that—with his presence, leadership, and organizational qualities—by aiming his energies at intimidating the druggies he could have cleaned up his whole neighborhood in one tenth the time.

Ed Powell, executive director of the Umma Group,[1] seated alongside Mr. Foster, was next to speak. Mr. Powell was a neatly dressed, soft-spoken, slim man in his mid-fifties, who, like Ice Foster, exuded a powerful presence without saying a word. In a soft, confident voice he described how his community organization had sharply reduced drug trafficking in an area covering two miles of some of the meanest, druggie-infested streets imaginable, with a citizens' patrol unit called the "Umma Patrol." As he described the dress, appearance, and how the patrol worked, I realized he was describing the basics of how a BAD patrol should look and function. The Umma Patrol, comprised of 150 men dressed in distinctive black berets and green camouflage uniforms, patrolled its community turf on foot and in clearly marked red vans. They carried walkie-talkie radios to communicate with each other and the local police, with whom they worked in a spirit of close cooperation.

"The police don't like to think a whole lot about it," said Mr. Powell. "When the stuff hits the fan, they know the good guys are wearing the [Umma patrol uniform]."

I found myself on the edge of my chair. This was exciting to me; a ray of hope. The only point where my philosophy and that of Mr. Powell seemed to differ was in the target of his operations—the brave souls of his organization hunted *drug dealers*. I raised my hand for the third time that day.

"Does your group make citizens' arrests?" I asked.

"Yes," said the calm, almost peacefully smiling man. "We do."

With that an irate middle-aged man in a crew haircut

[1] *Umma* is an Arabic word meaning "community."

representing a tenants' association from Co-op City in The Bronx stood and, sounding like every politician and bureaucrat I have ever heard, irately snapped, "Citizens' patrols are *never* to make arrests. That is for the police to do. We can be nothing more than the eyes and ears of the police, who are the professionals. . . ."

He rolled on at great length about the folly of a group of citizens trying to take police action, his angry, threatened voice dimming in my ears as I began to study the faces of those listening, realizing that most not only believed his words, but were comforted by them. They were words that excused citizens from taking action to save themselves, and for the responsibility of their own living environment. *That's someone else's job. I pay my taxes, don't I? I pay for police protection.*

I began to understand the man's fear and anger. I looked at Mr. Powell's face and noticed that he was listening with a small knowing smile, and a faint twinkle in his eyes. When the crew-cut man from Co-op City finished, no one had anything to say in rebuttal.

Late that afternoon, as I left the meeting, my head swirled with the enormity of the problem. How do you organize a country against an enemy it hasn't even recognized yet?

I hope this book is the beginning.

MY DAUGHTER

The phone woke me at three A.M., a couple of days before I finished the first draft of *Fight Back*. It was my daughter, Niki, now twenty-two and drug free for almost five years. The conversation we had was one that belongs in these pages.

"Daddy, I'm sorry, but I had to call you," said my

daughter, her words coming in a furious, clipped rush. "If I didn't have you to talk to, I don't know what I'd do," she said, now breaking into tears.

"Go ahead, baby, talk to me," I said, holding on to the phone with one hand, the other reflexively groping for my clothing and a gun and badge that were no longer there.

Earlier in the evening Niki had gone to a dance club with some of her friends and ran into an old neighbor of ours. "Harry" was a very successful businessman who was known among our mutual neighbors for having a very expensive cocaine habit that he could easily afford. His was the perfect profile for membership in the fattest part of our national demand for drugs—the soft market. Early in my career, during the years of my war against the dealers, I had avoided any contact with him and anyone like him. I was of the mind: *They are only hurting themselves; if they want to kill themselves, let them.* But I could not have been more wrong.

"That son of a bitch," said my daughter, her voice going shrill. "He stuck coke right in front of me."

"He offered you coke?" I started jamming the phone between chin and shoulder and pulling my pants on. Harry was one son of a bitch that was not going to see the sun rise.

"Yes," she said, and began sobbing. "I'm a recovering addict. Don't bastards like that know how hard it is?"

"Don't worry, baby. We'll do something about him."

"I want you to lock him up, Daddy."

"I'll take care of him, baby. I promise."

My daughter and I spoke for another hour or so, somehow managing to calm each other down. I realized that she had developed enough strength to resist the offer of drugs on her own, and only needed someone to talk to; thank God I was there. And she realized that as long as she loved me enough to show the kind of strength she had, I would always be there for her. If ever I needed evidence of her Choice of Love, it was right there in that phone call.

"You know, Daddy," she said finally, "people like Harry are worse than drug dealers."

"I know it, baby, but why are you saying it?"

"Well, because when I was a young kid and first experimenting, some of the dealers liked me and used to chase me away. One once told me, 'None of *us* use this shit, Niki. It's business. Do yourself a favor and don't get started.'

"I could understand them, Daddy. They did it for money. But druggies just do it for kicks. And they, more than anyone, know how hard it is to say no."

"Honey, how would you like to do something that might really help some people?" I said. In the past I had spoken about my daughter's "victory" against drug addiction on television and radio, but was never specific about our experience together, or what she had been through. She had always resisted the idea of "going public," and I respected her feelings. Just getting her approval for the section already included in the book had been tough enough.

"What?"

"Let me put this conversation and what happened to you in my book. I think it might help in getting people to start looking in the right direction."

"Do you really, Daddy?"

"I sure do."

"Then go ahead."

A couple of days later I was on the way to the post office to mail the manuscript to my editor, when I noticed a newspaper headline that sent me back to the word processor one final time.

IMAGINE NO DRUGS, said the headlines of the New York *Daily News,* in two-inch block letters. The words were excerpted from an essay written by fifth-grader, Eric Garcia, of East New York, a neighborhood that has been described as "more dangerous than Lebanon" due to its drug-related violence. In the words of young Eric:

> My Community would be a better place to live if it were "drug free." Families would enjoy normal, happy lives. Sons and daughters would be truthful to their parents. Babies would grow up to be healthy adults and grandparents would be pleased and proud to see their families united.[1]

Just imagine . . . a world without drugs.

---

[1] Mike McAlary, "A Bit of Hope from the Kids," New York *Daily News,* 10/12/90.

APPENDIX I

Data Every Citizen Should Know Concerning Common Drugs of Abuse

A. Cannabis Family of Drugs

DRUG	APPEARANCE	HOW USED	DEPENDENCY
Marijuana *Street Names: Pot, Grass, Reefer, Acapulco Gold, Skunk, Ditch Weed, Mary Jane, Sinsemilla, Sincie, Weed, Loco Weed, Joint, Dope, Jamaican, Sativa, Thai Sticks, Colombian*	Dried parsley with seeds	Smoked or eaten	Long-term use leads to *strong* psychological addiction MEDICAL USE: Experimental

DRUG	APPEAR-ANCE	HOW USED	DEPEN-DENCY
THC (Tetra-hydrocan-nabinol)	Soft gelatin capsules, or dark or amber liquid	Smoked or taken orally	" "
Hashish Street Names: Hash, Camel Shit, Hash Cakes	Brown, black, or tan cakes, balls, rocks, or rocky powder	Eaten or smoked	" "
Hashish oil Street Name: Hash Oil	Thick liquid varying from clear to dark in color	Smoked in tobacco or marijuana	" "

Behavioral Effects on User
Cannabis users usually appear lethargic, sleepy, and unco-ordinated. Their sense of the passage of time, short-term memory, and comprehension may be severely altered. The drug also induces extreme hunger urges and uncontrolled, inappropriate fits of laughter and giggling. The drug may also induce severe episodes of paranoia and psychosis. The user will suddenly become hyperactive, frightened, unable to sit still. He or she may have an overpowering fear that "something bad" is about to happen to them.

Physical Effects on User
According to DEA's literature marijuana contains more cancer-causing agents than cigarettes. The physical damage

done is exacerbated by the method of smoking—inhaling and holding the smoke in the lungs as deeply and as long as one can stand it. Generally it increases the heart rate, causes bloodshot eyes and dry throat and mouth. Other tests indicate that there is a good possibility that long-term use of cannabis may cause genetic damage.

Overdose effects can include fatigue, paranoia, psychotic episodes, hallucinations, rapid heartbeat, and high blood pressure.

Withdrawal effects can include insomnia, hyperactivity, decreased appetite, depression, and disorientation.

Personal Observation

Most habitual marijuana users I have known over a period of time seem to pay a heavy, permanent price in terms of energy, motivation, and intellectual capacity.

Field Test

Cannabis may mimic other drugs. A quick field test that may determine whether or not an individual had recently smoked is the onion test. If a piece of raw onion is available, squeeze and mash it just beneath the subject's nose. If no tears come to his eyes, it is a good indication that he or she has recently smoked marijuana or ingested some other member of the cannabis family.

B. Derivatives of the Coca Leaf

DRUG	APPEAR-ANCE	HOW USED	ADDICTIVE CHARAC-TERISTICS
Cocaine *Street Names: Coke, Toot, Flake, Crystal, Snow, Blow, Lady, Girl, White Lady, Nose Candy, Perico, Powder, White, Caine*	White crystal powder —color may vary to off-white	Inhaled through nasal passages, smoked, and injected	Extremely addictive, characterized by a quickly developing tolerance MEDICAL USE: Local anesthetic
Crack cocaine *Street Names: Crack, Freebase Rocks, Rock*	Tan or beige rocky powder or pellet —or crystalline rocks resembling caked soap powder, usually packaged in small plastic vials	Smoked in special pipes, constructed of glass, metal, or plastic	Extremely addictive, with user developing a rapid tolerance to the drug MEDICAL USE: none
Coca paste *Street*	Beige or gray powder	Smoked mixed with	Same as cocaine

Names: Ba-	either to-	**MEDICAL**
zooka, Pichi-	bacco or	**USE:** none
cata, Base,	marijuana	
Coca Base		

Behavioral Effects of Cocaine
Cocaine is a powerful stimulant of the central nervous system. The behavior will vary, depending on the length of time the user has been ingesting the drug and how heavily addicted he or she has become. Early in the addictive process the user will appear euphoric, animated, extremely talkative, and energetic. As the drug wears off the user will appear as though his battery has worn down. He will withdraw into a shell, become less talkative, and sullen and depressed, until the next opportunity to ingest more cocaine. Each time the drug is taken the period of euphoria grows shorter and the period of depression longer and more pronounced, until the user is taking the drug mainly to stave off the depression. At the beginning of a user's addictive process the effects of the drug may last as long as a half hour to an hour. After heavy use (over a period of hours), the drug's effects may last no longer than five or ten minutes.

Thus, in a social situation, one of the constants of all cocaine users is the frequency with which they must leave the room—making frequent trips to the bathroom, or outside to "get some air"—and equally frequent and corresponding mood swings. You may also notice, among users who inhale cocaine, a frequently stuffed and running nose.

Physical Effects of Cocaine
The drug is a powerful stimulant to the central nervous system. It quickly increases heart rate, respiratory rate, body temperature, and blood pressure. It causes sweating, headaches, blurred vision, insomnia, and decreased appetite.

It may cause severe physical tremors, seizures, and/or instant death by disrupting the brain's control over the heart and respiration. Inhaling it through the nostrils will damage the mucous membrane, causing prolonged bouts of stuffy nose and, in cases of chronic and frequent use, the ulceration of the nasal membrane until it is completely perforated.

Overdose effects can include an increase in body temperature, hallucinations, convulsions, heart attack, stroke, coma, and death.

Withdrawal symptoms may include apathy, irritability, mild to profound depression, disorientation, and long periods of sleep.

Personal Observation

In my twenty-five years of undercover work for four federal agencies, I have had occasion to spend an extensive amount of time among drug users. Among all the drugs available cocaine (in its various forms) is easily the most violence inducing. It is also the drug of choice for most Americans, which perhaps best explains why America leads the rest of the world—by far—in all statistics of crimes of violence.

C. Chemical and Pharmaceutical Stimulants

DRUG	APPEARANCE	HOW USED	ADDICTIVE CHARACTERISTICS
Amphetamines *Medical names:* Benzedrine, Dexedrine,	Capsules, pills, tablets, and powder	Taken orally, injected, and inhaled through nasal passages	Extremely addictive; cocaine and amphetamines are the only

Bisome-mine, Delcobese, Desoxyn, Mediatric *Street Names: Speed, Black Beauties, Pep Pills, Bumblebees, Hearts, Footballs, Uppers, Ups, Copilots*

drugs that animals will self-administer until they die MEDICAL USES: weight reduction, narcolepsy, and hyperkinesis

DRUG	APPEARANCE	HOW USED	ADDICTIVE QUALITIES
Methamphetamines: Methedrine *Street Names: Ice, Blue Ice, Crank Meth, Crystal, Meth Speed*	Powder, pills, and a rock resembling a block of paraffin or waxlike substance	Injected, taken orally, or inhaled through the nasal passages like cocaine	See Amphetamines MEDICAL USE: none

DRUG	APPEARANCE	HOW USED	ADDICTIVE CHARACTERISTICS
Other Stimulants: Cylert, Didrex, Plegine, Pre-Sate, Preluden, Ritalin, Sanorex, Tenuate, Tepanil, Voranil	Pills, capsules, and tablets— some users will crush to powder form	Taken orally and injected	Extremely addictive, with a rapidly increasing tolerance MEDICAL USES: Weight control, narcolepsy, hyperkinesis

Behavioral Effects of Stimulant Drugs

The effects are similar to those noted in cocaine users, perhaps even more pronounced. The superanimation noted is best expressed by the street term *speeding,* used to describe someone under the effects of methamphetamine (speed). Users appear restless (unable to sit still), inattentive, dry mouthed, anxious, moody; may even appear psychotic.

Physical Effects of Stimulant Drugs

Increased heart rate, blood pressure, and respiration, dilated pupils, and decreased appetite. Users may also experience severe headaches, sweating, blurred vision, dizziness, sleeplessness, and severe anxiety. Prolonged use may lead to bouts of paranoia, hallucinations, and delusions—amphetamine psychosis. Heavy amphetamine users will often suffer large, unsightly skin blemishes and ulcers.

Overdose effects: agitation, increase in body temperature, convulsions, hallucinations, which may end in a stroke or heart failure and death.

Withdrawal symptoms may include apathy, irritability, depression, disorientation, loss of appetite, and long periods of sleep.

Personal Observation

Many users find stimulant drugs the drug of choice when cocaine is not available. As John Lawn, ex-administrator of the Drug Enforcement Administration, predicted, different brands of stimulant drugs, like Blue Ice, may become the drugs to replace cocaine should we ever succeed in controlling South American cocaine production. At last count, speed (according to Drug Enforcement Administration figures), was a $3-billion-dollar-a-year business and growing—and all of it grown right here in the good old U.S.A.

D. Chemical and Pharmaceutical Depressants

DRUG	APPEARANCE	HOW USED	ADDICTIVE CHARACTERISTICS
Barbiturates: Amytal, Butisol, Doriden, Fiorinal, Lotusate, Nembutal, Phenobarbital, Seconal	Red, yellow, blue, or red-and-blue capsules	Orally	Moderately to highly addictive, both physically and psychologically MEDICAL USES: anesthetic, anticonvulsant, sedative, hypnotic

DRUG	APPEAR-ANCE	HOW USED	ADDICTIVE CHARAC-TERISTICS
Street Names: Downers, Barbs, Blues, Reds, Blue Devils, Red Devils, Yellows, Yellow Jackets			
Chloral Hydrate: Noctec	Orange gelatin capsules	Taken orally	Moderately addictive, both physically and psychologically MEDICAL USE: Hypnotic
Benzodiazepines *(Tranquilizers):* Ativan, Dalmane, Diazepam, Halcion, Librium, Valium, Versed, Verstran, Xanax	Pills and capsules	Taken orally	Not considered highly addictive either physically or psychologically (according to the Drug Enforcement Administration litera-

ture)[1]
MEDICAL
USES: anti-
anxiety,
anticonvul-
sant, seda-
tive, hyp-
notic

Personal Observation
While this type of depressant is not listed as "highly addictive" in the Drug Enforcement Administration literature, I
have known too many people heavily addicted to some of
the above-listed substances to place much faith in the rating.

DRUG	APPEAR-ANCE	HOW USED	ADDICTIVE CHARAC-TERISTICS
Metha-qualone: Quaalude, Sopor *Street Names: Ludes, Buis-cuits, Lulus, Soapers*	White pill, similar to aspirin	Taken orally	Highly ad-dictive both physically and psycho-logically MEDICAL USES: seda-tive, hyp-notic

NOTE:
This drug is extremely dangerous in that for some users the
physical tolerance does not grow as fast as the need for

[1] *Drugs of Abuse,* 1988 Edition, Department of Justice, Drug Enforcement Administration.

more of the drug to achieve a feeling of high. Thus the amount needed to make the next satisfactory high may be enough to kill the user.

Glute-thimide: Doriden	White pill, similar to aspirin	Taken orally	Highly addictive physically and moderately addictive psychologically MEDICAL USES: sedative, hypnotic
Other depressants: Equanil, Miltown, Noludar, Placidyl, Valmid	Pills and capsules	Taken orally	Moderately addictive, both physically and psychologically MEDICAL USES: anxiety, depression, sedative, hypnotic

Behavioral Effect on User
The barbiturate druggie will give the outward appearance of being drunk—without the odor of alcohol—appearing sleepy, disoriented, with slurred speech and poor coordination.

Physical Effects on User
Prolonged use of depressants builds a tolerance and makes larger and larger doses necessary to achieve a high. An overdose can cause respiratory depression, coma, and death. Use of alcohol with depressants greatly increases the effect of the drugs and the risk of overdose and death. Pregnant mothers abusing depressant drugs also run the risk of addicting their unborn babies.

Overdose effects include widely dilated pupils, weak and rapid pulse, clammy skin, shallow respiration, coma, and death.

Withdrawal symptoms ranging from restlessness, insomnia, and anxiety to severe convulsive seizures and possibly death. These types of drugs are perhaps the most dangerous to withdraw from without medical supervision.

E. Hallucinogenic Drugs

DRUG	APPEARANCE	HOW USED	DEPENDENCY
Lysergic Acid Diethylamide: LSD *Street Names: Acid, Green or Red Dragon, Dots, Microdots, Lucy, Blue Lady, Blue Heaven,*	Clear liquid that may be used to impregnate sugar cubes, blotter paper, candy, or may be in pill or capsule form	Taken orally, with an eye dropper, licked off blotter paper	Not considered physically addictive— psychological dependency is unknown MEDICAL USE: Experimental

DRUG	APPEAR-ANCE	HOW USED	ADDICTIVE CHARAC-TERISTICS
Cubes, Sugar Cubes			
Phencyclidine: PCP *Street Names: Angel Dust, Hog, Dust*	Liquid, pills, capsules, white crystalline powder	Injected, taken orally, smoked, may be sprayed on tobacco, marijuana, food	The physical dependence factor is unknown; however, PCP is considered highly addictive, psychologically MEDICAL USE: Veterinary anesthetic

Personal Observation

On the street angel dust is considered one of the more potent violence- and paranoia-inducing drugs. I have seen "dusted" druggies undergo seizurelike episodes of violence, during which they inflicted serious damage on themselves and people around them.

DRUG	APPEAR-ANCE	HOW USED	ADDICTIVE CHARAC-TERISTICS
Amphetamine Variants: DMA,	Liquid capsules, pills, powder	May be snorted, sniffed, in-	Officially, it is unknown whether or

STP, PMA, MDA, TMA, DOM, DOB (Chemical variations of Mexcallin and Amphetamine) *Street Names: Serenity, Tranquility, Peace*		jected, taken orally, and licked off impregnated blotter paper	not this type of drug is either physically or psychologically addictive. MEDICAL USE: none
Mescaline and Peyote *Street Names: Mesc, Buttons, Peyote, Cactus, Dream Buttons*	Hard brown discs, tablets, capsules	Tablets and capsules are taken orally; discs are chewed, swallowed, or smoked	Not believed to be physically addictive. It is unknown whether the drug is psychologically addictive MEDICAL USE: none
Psilocybin *Street Names: Magic Mushroom, Mushroom, Magic M,*	Fresh or dried mushrooms	Chewed and swallowed	Not believed to be physically addictive. It is unknown whether the drug is psy-

DRUG	APPEAR-ANCE	HOW USED	ADDICTIVE CHARAC-TERISTICS
Dream Mushroom, Silly Sy			chologically addictive MEDICAL USE: none

Behavioral Effects of Hallucinogens on Users

Users—particularly of LSD, mescaline, and psilocybin—experience visual and aural hallucinations and appear to be in "another world." Psychiatrists originally believed that LSD mimicked schizophrenia. Under the influence a user's coordination can be described as poor to nonexistent. In instances called "bad trips" the user may appear in a state of extreme panic and terror, oftentimes overcome with a fear of imminent death.

Physical Effects of Hallucinogens on Users

In general, physical effects may include increased heart rate, blood pressure, and respiration, loss of appetite, sleeplessness, and tremors. Users of LSD, mescaline, and psilocybin may experience flashbacks (recurring effects of drugs) long after use has been discontinued.

Overdose Effects

Longer, more intense "trip" episodes, permanent psychosis and mental impairment, convulsions, coma, heart and lung failure, death.

F. Narcotic Drugs

DRUG DE-PENDENCY	APPEARANCE	HOW USED	ADDICTIVE CHARACTRISTICS
Heroin *Street Names: Horse, Smack, Boy, Junk, Dope, Teca, Manteca, H, Big H, Shit, Dragon, Mexican Brown, China White, Elephant Brand, Dragon Brand*	White, beige, or brown powder, sold on street in small glassine envelopes, sometimes marked with a brand name (e.g., "DOA")	Injected, sniffed, and smoked	Highly addictive, both physically and psychologically MEDICAL USE: In U.S., none
Opium: Dover's Powder, Paregoric, Parepectolin *Street Names: Black Gum, Tar, Dream Tar, Dream Smoke*	Dark brown chunks, dark brown tarlike substance, powder	Taken orally and smoked	Highly addictive, both physically and psychologically MEDICAL USE: Analgesic and antidiarrheal

Morphine: Brand Names: MS-Contin, Roxanol, Roxanal-SR *Street Name: Dr. Morpheus*	White crystals, injectable solutions, tablets	Taken orally, smoked, and injected	Highly addictive, both physically and psychologically MEDICAL USE: analgesic and antitussive
Codeine: Brand and trade names: Empirin w/ Codeine, Fiorinal w/ Codeine, Robitussin A-C, Tylenol w/Codeine *Street Names: Cody, GI Gin, Deen, Code Dee*	Dark liquid, capsules and tablets resembling aspirin	Taken orally and injected	Highly addictive both physically and psychologically MEDICAL USE: Analgesic and antitussive
Hydromorphone: Trade name: Dilaudid *Street Names:*	Tablet and liquid injectable form	Taken oral and injected	Highly addictive both physically and psychologically MEDICAL

Dilly-doo,   USE: analge-
Laudie   sic

Personal Observation
The effects of Dilaudid are shorter lasting than those of morphine but much more sedating, and it is believed to be from two to eight times more potent. It is much sought after by narcotic addicts and is usually obtained through fraudulent prescriptions or drugstore robberies.

DRUG	APPEARANCE	HOW USED	ADDICTIVE CHARACTERISTICS
Methadone: Brand and trade names: Dolophine, Methadone, Methadose *Street Names:* Meth, Liquid Meth	Liquid and tablets	Taken orally and injected	High-physical, low-psychological MEDICAL USE: analgesic
Meperidine (Pethidine): Trade or brand names: Demerol, Mepergan	White powder, solution, and tablets	Taken orally and injected	Highly addictive, both physically and psychologically MEDICAL USE: analgesic

Other Nar-cotics: Darvon, Lomotil, Talwin, Percocet, Percodan, Tussionex, Tylox, Fentanyl	Capsules, tablets, liq-uid	Taken orally and injected	High-physi-cal, low-psy-chological MEDICAL USES: Anal-gesic, anti-diarrheal, anitussive

Behavioral Effects of Narcotic Drugs

Lethargy, euphoria, drowsiness, slurred speech, drooping of the eyelids, constricted pupils, watery eyes, at times itching. Heroin users, in particular, will be observed seated for long periods of time, their chins drooped to their chests, in a posture known on the street as "nodding." As drug wears off, yawning, itching, and watery eyes will be increasingly apparent, leading—if no drugs are obtained—to full with-drawal symptoms.

Physical Effects

Narcotic drugs depress the central nervous system, slow res-piration and heartbeat, and lower blood pressure.

Effects of Overdose

Shallow respiration, clammy skin, weak and rapid pulse, convulsions, coma, and death.

Withdrawal

Watery eyes, runny nose, yawning, severe itching and cramps, nausea, tremors, chills, sweating, panic attacks, loss of appetite. Withdrawal from narcotic drugs should be done under medical supervision.

G. Inhalants

DRUG DE-PENDENCY	APPEAR-ANCE	HOW USED	ADDICTIVE CHARAC-TERISTICS
Gasoline, Airplane Glue, Paint Thinner, Dry-Cleaner Fluid	Commercial jars and cans	Soaked in rags and inhaled, or inhaled directly from containers or plastic and paper bags	Psychologically addictive

Behavioral Effects of Narcotic Drugs
Extremely violence inducing; users sometimes appear drunk, with extremely impaired coordination; frequently causes nausea and vomiting.

Physical Effects
Users often show a drastic weight loss, brain, liver, and bone-marrow damage, frequently suffering memory loss and impaired vision.

Effects of Overdose
There is an extremely high risk of sudden death.

APPENDIX II
Drug–World Glossary

After a few years in narcotics enforcement I began to realize that I was no longer in an occupation; I had entered a subworld, the inhabitants of which are the druggies, the law (street narcs and cops, a few individual defense lawyers and prosecutors), and the suppliers (from street dealers to smugglers). The drug world has its own language, rules, and hierarchy. For a community organization to be successful in conquering that world, it must first make itself part of it; and an important part of doing so is to learn its language.

Acapulco gold—a potent brand of marijuana grown in Mexico, noted by its yellowish tint.

ADA—assistant district attorney.

angel dust—a hallucinogenic drug (see Appendix I).

angel off—This is an old narcotics enforcement term that refers to keeping a drug den under observation and arresting the drug buyers—after they have their drugs and have traveled a sufficient distance from the dealer

—so that the arrest will not affect the dealer's operation.

AUSA—assistant United States attorney.

bad—tough; mean; cool; slick; very, very good.

base—cocaine base; cocaine in its simplest form, before crystallization into its final form—cocaine hydrocholoride. This is a smokable form of cocaine and is the forerunner of crack.

big C—cocaine, or crack.

biscuit—Quaalude, methaqualone (see Appendix I).

black beauty—stimulant drug (see Appendix I).

blasted—state of extreme intoxication.

blitzed—high on drugs.

blow—cocaine, or a dose of cocaine.

bong—a pipe, similar to a water pipe, used for smoking marijuana.

bundle—a quantity of street heroin, usually twenty-five bags.

burn, or, to be burned—sell phony drugs as the real thing; be recognized as an undercover police officer. As a noun: recognition of a surveillance by a drug criminal; an action by an undercover officer that reveals to suspects that they are under surveillance and/or investigation.

bust—an arrest.

buy/bust—an undercover operation wherein the undercover agent, posing as a drug buyer, shows the drug dealer money, pretending to make the buy, but instead arrests him.

carburetor—a marijuana pipe with an extra hole allowing one person to blow while the other inhales, allegedly increasing the impact of the drug.

carrying—"Is he or she carrying?" refers to whether or not an individual has drugs or a gun on his person.

chota—street Spanish for informer.

Christmas Trees—amphetamine drugs.

class-one case—In DEA the "quality" of a case is denoted by class—class one, two, three, or four—the top-quality drug case being class one.

coke—cocaine.

collar—arrest.

colorless, odorless ice—see *ice.*

come-down—the wearing off of the effects of drugs.

con job—a phony story or set of facts.

connection—a drug dealer, or a source of drugs.

cop—(v) to buy drugs; to steal or otherwise obtain; (n) police.

crack—cocaine in its basic, primary state, when it is smokable.

crack head—crack addict.

crank—combination of crack and heroin, usually smoked; also used to refer to crystal meth (see Appendix I under "Stimulants").

crystal meth—stimulant drug (see Appendix I).

DA—district attorney.

DEA—Drug Enforcement Administration.

dealing—selling drugs; on the street usually refers to users selling to each other.

dibbing and dabbing—experimenting with drugs, as a novice; taking drugs infrequently, on weekends and at parties.

ditch weed—marijuana.

dime someone out—to inform on someone.

dirty—having drugs, guns, or drug money on one's person.

doobies—marijuana joints.

dope—on the street, was historically used to refer to heroin; as of late, marijuana as well.

drop a dime—inform on someone.

druggie—any drug consumer, buyer, or addict.

dust—angel dust, PCP, a strong hallucinogenic substance.

dusted—high on angel dust. Extremely dangerous, psychotic condition during which the user is capable of extreme violence.

ecstasy—an amphetamine derivative (see Appendix I, under amphetamine).

flake—cocaine; also, the act of placing drugs on a suspect's person—usually done by corrupt law-enforcement officers, who subsequently arrest and charge the individual with possession of those drugs.

flip—to convert an arrested person into an informant; to convince an arrested person to testify against his co-defendants.

freak—street term for someone who looks and acts the part of a druggie.

freak-out—violent, wild, or angry reaction; a bad trip on drugs.

free-basing—another method of reducing cocaine to a smokable form causing an extremely quick and intense high similar to that of crack.

garbage head—a drug addict who will ingest, or inject into his or her body, just about any substance imaginable. Garbage heads are considered the lowest of the low among addicts.

grass—marijuana.

get paid—to rob.

girl—cocaine.

hash—hashish

hash oil—the superpotent oily extract of hashish.

hassle—a difficult time; difficulty; a problem.

head—a druggie who is continuously high on drugs.

heat—police; surveillance; a gun.

herb—marijuana.

hit—a mob rubout; an arrest; the signal given by police for a raid or arrest; a toke on a marijuana joint or crack pipe; a drug injection.

homegrown—domestically grown marijuana.

horse—heroin (see Appendix I).

ice—the street name for crystallized methamphetamine. Considered likely to be the replacement drug for crack, should the cocaine war ever be won.

J—marijuana joint.

jive, jiving—see "con."

joint—marijuana cigarette; jail.

jump collar—a spur-of-the-moment drug arrest for a violation committed in the arresting officer's presence or view.

junkie—addict; usually refers to heroin addiction, although lately it is coming into use to describe crack and cocaine addicts.

key—a kilo (1,000 grams; 2.2 pounds). Drugs of a foreign origin are usually sold by this measure.

lid—about an ounce of marijuana.

love drug—crack, cocaine.

magic mushroom—psilocybin (see Appendix I).

man, the—usually refers to the police; might be used to refer to a drug connection or a drug dealer.

Mary Jane—slang for marijuana.

media mileage—a term used by the drug-war bureaucrats to describe the amount of media coverage an investigation might bring them.

mescaline—hallucinogenic drug (see Appendix I).

mix—substances used to dilute heroin, cocaine, and other narcotics found in a powder form.

narc—a law-enforcement officer involved in narcotics enforcement.

OP—observation post.

OZ—an ounce quantity of drugs.

papers—marijuana rolling papers.

party—when druggies say *party* they mean "get high."

PC—probable cause. Sufficient legal grounds to believe a crime has been committed, or that contraband is being hidden in a particular location. Search-and-arrest warrants are issued on the basis of sufficient probable cause.

PCP—angel dust (see Appendix I).

piece—usually means a gun. It may be used to refer to a quantity of drugs.

pigs—police.

plea bargain, or plea-bargain agreement—an agreement between a prosecuting attorney and an arrested defendant, during which the defendant is usually sentenced to a lesser term in jail in exchange for a guilty plea.

pot—marijuana.

perico—previously, a Colombian slang word meaning cocaine. Now coming into more common use by us gringos.

Peruvian flake—cocaine.

quality case—in the lexicon of narcotics agents and prosecuting attorneys, this refers to cases involving either large drug seizures or big-name violators, resulting in a lot of media attention.

rainbows—LSD on paper.

reefer—marijuana.

resin—residue of marijuana left in pipe after smoking, which contains a high level of THC.

rip-off—a robbery during a drug exchange. The common fear of druggies and dealers and undercover cops.

ripped—high on drugs.

roach—druggie, drug buyer, addict.

roach clip—metal clip used to hold marijuana joint while smoking it down to a stub.

rocks—cocaine or crack.

roller—young street dealer usually seen wearing baseball cap and "beeper."

ROR—"released on own recognizance," indicating that an arrested defendant has been released without bail, on his word to return to court for his next hearing.

rush—an intense feeling experienced on ingesting a drug; amyl nitrite, a street drug sold in small brown bottles that are broken and inhaled, giving the user a fast sixty-second high.

SAC—special agent in charge of a DEA or FBI office.

script—prescription paper, stolen or counterfeit, used to illegally obtain prescription drugs from pharmacies.

set, the—is a theatrical term that both law enforcement and habitués of the drug world have adapted to mean "the street" at any given time or location. (e.g., "Is he on the set?")

shadow—follow; put under surveillance.

sheesh—hashish.

shit—drugs.

shoot up—inject drugs with a hypodermic needle.

'shrooms—magic mushroom (see Appendix I).

sinsemilla—a relatively new and superpotent brand of marijuana. Also: sinse; seedless.

skunk—marijuana.

smack—heroin.

smoke—marijuana.

snitch—informant.

snow—cocaine; also, to lie or deceive.

SOP—standard operating procedure.

speed, speeders—amphetamine (see Appendix I).

speedball—cocaine or crack, mixed with heroin, either injected or smoked.

stash—hidden storehouses of drugs and, possibly, money.

steerer—a street go-between who "steers" prospective buyers to sellers for a commission; usually drugs.

stoned—high on drugs.

stool—stool pigeon, informer.

straight—(adj) sober; clean; off drugs; (n) a non–drug user.

subject—a defendant, a suspect, or a target of an investigation.

suit—law-enforcement administrative type, as opposed to a "street" agent, or enforcement officer.

SNEU—street narcotics enforcement unit. Special enforcement units formed in each of New York City's numerous police precincts for the purpose of cleaning up street sales of narcotics.

snort—cocaine, or, the act of inhaling cocaine.

tail—follow.

Thai stick—a potent brand of marijuana grown in the Far East.

THC—tetrahydrocanabinol, the chemical ingredient in marijuana causing the "high"; extracted and sold in capsule form.

time served—a jail sentence wherein an arrested defendant is immediately released, the "time served" being the time he spent in jail awaiting, and during, trial.

toot—cocaine.

toss—police jargon meaning *stop and frisk* or *search*.

Trojan horse—a police undercover technique wherein an undercover officer driving a van buys drugs from a street dealer and at the moment of sale officers hidden in the rear jump out and arrest the dealer.

vitamin C—cocaine.

vitamin D—LSD.

vitamin H—heroin.

vitamin Q—Quaalude.

wasted—high on drugs.

weasel—informer.

weed—marijuana.

wise guy—member of organized crime.

works—hypodermic needle, syringe, and spoon used by addicts who inject drugs.

yellow jacket—amphetamine drug (see Appendix I).

zee—an ounce quantity of a drug.